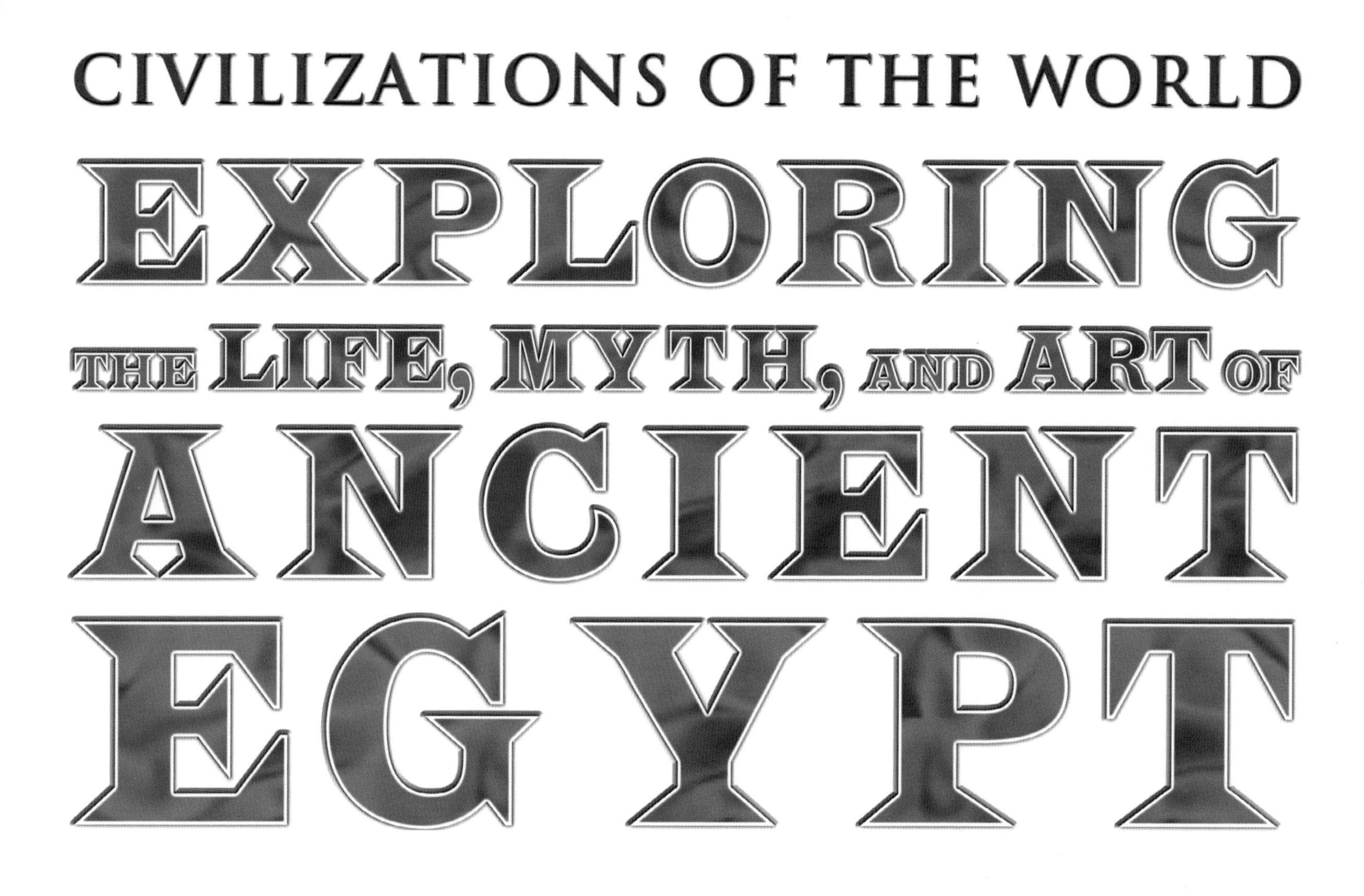

CIVILIZATIONS OF THE WORLD

EXPLORING THE LIFE, MYTH, AND ART OF ANCIENT EGYPT

JOANN FLETCHER

ROSEN PUBLISHING
New York

1/10

This edition published in 2010 by:

The Rosen Publishing Group, Inc.
29 East 21st Street
New York, NY 10010

Cover design by Matthew Cauli.

Library of Congress Cataloging-in-Publication Data

Fletcher, J. (Joann)
Exploring the life, myth, and art of ancient Egypt / Joann Fletcher.
p. cm.—(Civilizations of the world)
Includes index.
ISBN-13: 978-1-4358-5616-5 (Library binding)
1. Egypt—Civilization—To 332 B.C.—Juvenile literature. 2. Egypt—Social life and customs—To 332 B.C.—Juvenile literature. 3. Egypt—Antiquities—Juvenile literature. I. Title.
DT61.F583 2010
932—dc22

2009008792

Manufactured in Malaysia

CONTENTS

Image and Imagination

LEFT Rising from the sands on the fringe of the great Western Desert, the 4th-dynasty pyramids of Giza, near modern Cairo, are the most potent and unmistakable monuments of ancient Egyptian civilization, linking the earth and the sky in a royal stairway to the heavens.

The civilization of ancient Egypt was largely the product of its geography, particularly its river, the Nile. Egyptians called their country Kemet, "Black Land," which refers to the strip of fertile riverbank, bounded by Deshret, "Red Land," the vast, sterile desert. The dominant colors of the Egyptian world—blue skies, golden sun, red desert, green river margins, black, silt-laden Nile—are the chief hues of Egyptian art, which also reflects the layers of river, field, desert, and sky. This world existed in a state of equilibrium, of finely balanced opposites: Kemet and Deshret, day and night, life and death, order and chaos.

BELOW The falcon-headed sun god, Re-Harakhty, is depicted receiving the pharaoh Sety I (ca. 1290–1279 BCE). The prevalent blues, yellows, reds, and blacks of this painted relief scene are inspired by the colors of the Egyptian landscape.

THE SOUL OF ANCIENT EGYPT

The Egyptians believed that the balance of order and chaos in the universe could only be maintained by the gods and goddesses and their representative on earth, the king. Originally, these deities simply represented aspects of the natural world—the sun, the sky, the land, and the river—until each gradually developed a more complex personality and history as every area of the country embellished the stories and myths surrounding its own local deity. Eventually, many divinities came to share titles and attributes, and thus emerged the highly sophisticated pattern of religious belief that was so characteristic of ancient Egypt.

The divine forces required constant replenishment through worship if they were to guarantee the continuity of the cosmic equilibrium. Consequently, they were honored in repeated portrayals that adorn everything from monumental temples to delicate works of art. But it was above all in the performance of daily rites in the temples that the Egyptians venerated their deities. The temples were "storehouses" for divine power, which was maintained and directed by the priesthood for the good of the whole country. The high priest—always delegating for the king, the child of the gods—acted as intermediary between the mortal and divine worlds. He and his fellow priests and priestesses honored the deities with a constant stream of offerings, music, and dance, which was believed to encourage the divine spirit to reside within the temple—essential if the cosmic order was to be upheld.

LEFT The goddess of the sycamore tree (right) presents water to the dead man Kamose who kneels in front of her to make an offering to the divine triad—Osiris, Isis, and Horus—and Hathor. The limestone stela was made during the 20th dynasty ca. 1200 BCE.

RIGHT The Great Sphinx embodies the divine forces of royal power as it crouches protectively in the midst of the Giza necropolis. Originally built as a portrait of King Khafre of the 4th dynasty, this massive monument came to be regarded by many as a manifestation of the sun god.

THE STORY OF ANCIENT EGYPT

From the prehistoric cultures of the Nile valley two opposing kingdoms emerged, one in the north (Lower Egypt) and one in the south (Upper Egypt). They were unified ca. 3100 BCE by King Narmer at the start of the "Archaic Period." This was the early part of the "Old Kingdom," the name given to the first phase of Egyptian civilization. Narmer's successors established their base at Memphis (near modern Cairo), and organized the country through a highly efficient bureaucracy.

These early rulers created enough wealth to fund ambitious building schemes, culminating in the great pyramid complexes of Khufu, Khafre (4th dynasty), and other kings. But centuries of pyramid building drained the economy and central authority broke down ca. 2130 BCE. The Old Kingdom was followed by the "First Intermediate Period," in which the absence of a powerful political center is reflected in a lack of artistic standardization and idiosyncratic provincial art styles.

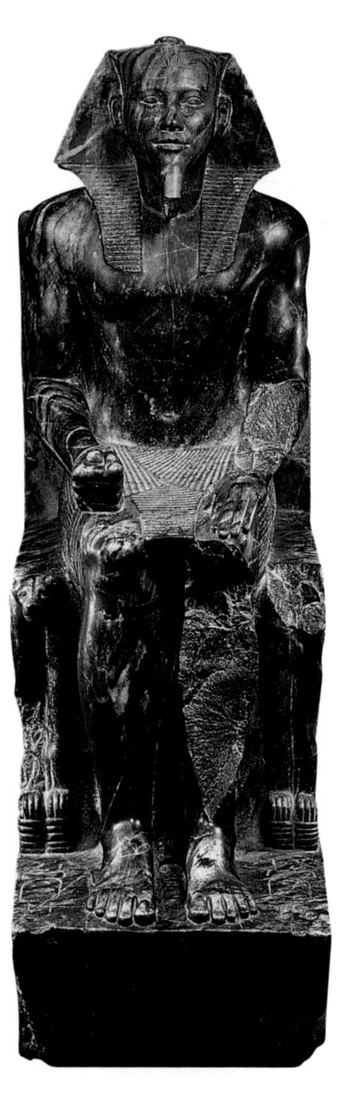

LEFT One of the artistic masterworks of the Old Kingdom is this superb diorite statue of King Khafre (ca. 2555–2532 BCE), son of Khufu and builder of the second of the three great pyramids of Giza. It was found in Khafre's valley temple, near his pyramid.

Egypt was reunited ca. 2000 BCE by princes of Thebes in the south, who inaugurated the "Middle Kingdom." Under the kings of the 11th and 12th dynasties (ca. 2108–1759 BCE), Thebes and its god, Amun, gained in importance, royal power was centralized, and Egypt's frontiers were expanded. In terms of art, language, and literature, the Middle Kingdom is regarded as ancient Egypt's "Classical Age."

Princes of Asiatic (Palestinian) origin known as the Hyksos ("Rulers of Foreign Lands") took control of the north ca. 1640 BCE and for a century (the "Second Intermediate Period") Egypt was split, with native Thebans ruling in the south. The country was reunited ca. 1530 BCE under another Theban dynasty, marking the start of the New Kingdom. A succession of warrior-pharaohs created a great empire, stretching from Nubia to the Euphrates, and Egypt became the richest and most powerful country in the ancient world. As in earlier ages, much of Egypt's wealth was channeled into great building projects to enhance the prestige of deities and kings. New

THE ANCIENT EGYPTIAN WORLD

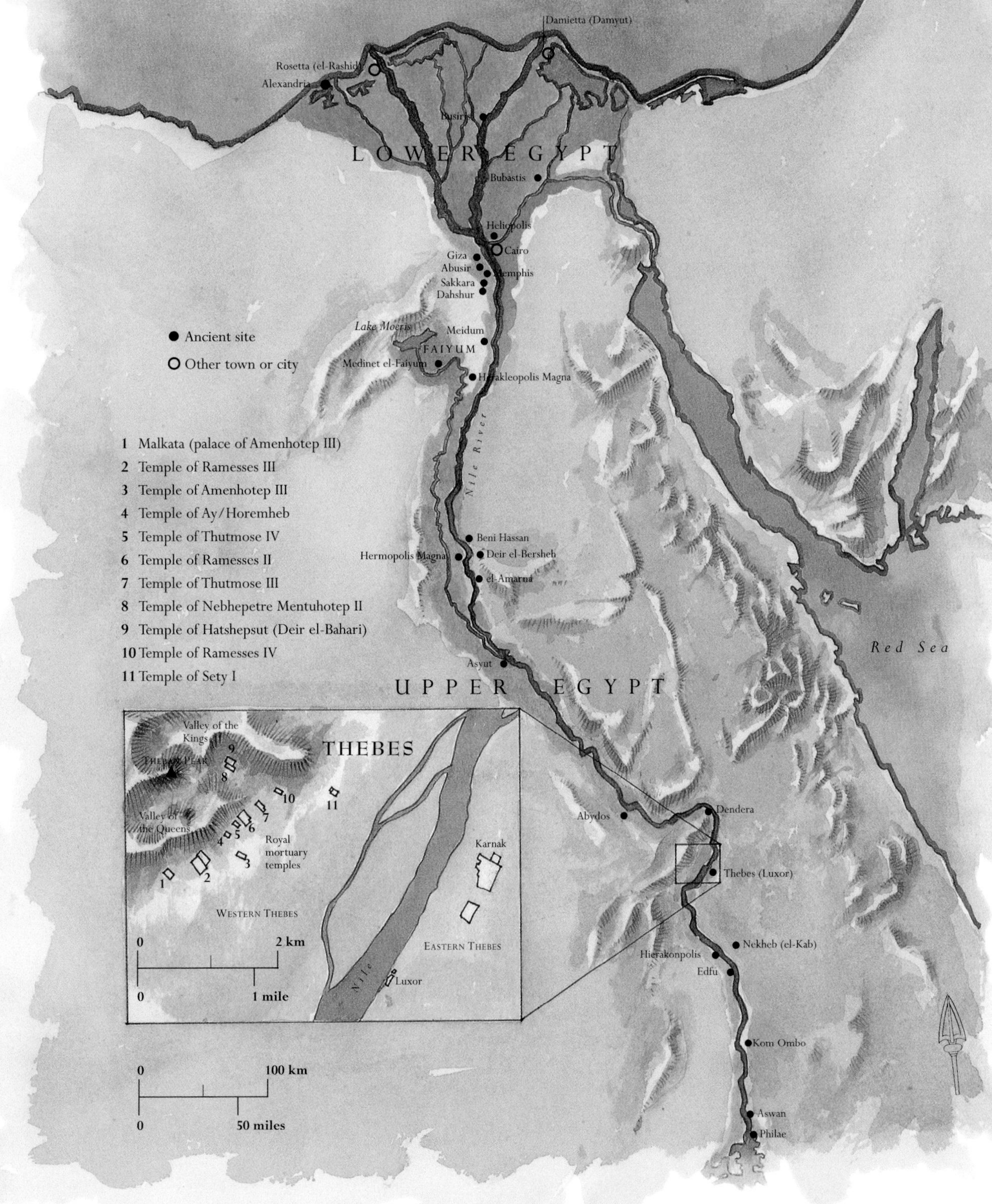

Kingdom pharaohs embellished the temple of Amun at Karnak, and built temples and tombs for themselves across the river.

Artistic and architectural achievement reached a peak under Amenhotep III (ca. 1390–1353 BCE), but his son Akhenaten (ca. 1353– 1335 BCE) destabilized the country during the "Amarna period" (see page 50). Akhenaten's short-lived successors—including his son Tutankhamun—gave way to an ex-general, Horemheb (ca. 1319–1292 BCE), who began to restore Egypt's fortunes.

LEFT **This exquisite 18th-dynasty funerary mask depicts the lady Thuya, the mother-in-law of King Amenhotep III and great-grandmother of Tutankhamun. It is made of gilded cartonnage inlaid with semiprecious stones and glass. Thuya's smiling features reflect those of Amenhotep himself (see illustration on page 50).**

ABOVE **A scene from the mortuary temple of the female pharaoh Hatshepsut (ca. 1479–1458 BCE) in western Thebes showing part of an Egyptian trade mission to east Africa. In their monuments, New Kingdom rulers depicted endless trade expeditions, military campaigns, and acts of worship—all intended to demonstrate their competence to rule.**

Horemheb was followed by the "Ramesside" kings of the 19th and 20th dynasties (ca. 1292–1075 BCE)—eleven of whom bore the famous name of Ramesses. Egypt kept its powerful position in the face of invasions by Mediterranean migrants and Libyans. But Libyan settlers seized the north ca. 1075 BCE and the New Kingdom finally collapsed. Only after four centuries of fragmentation (the "Third Intermediate Period") was the country reunited ca. 750 BCE by Nubian kings, who were succeeded by a final era of native rule (ca. 664–525 BCE).

From then on, Egypt was governed almost without interruption by successive foreign invaders. Persians (525–332 BCE) and Greeks (332–30 BCE) ruled in the traditional pharaonic way and the country's ancient culture remained largely intact. The Romans who followed (from 30 BCE) were absentee rulers, but they continued to endorse the old culture and religion—until 392 CE, when the empire officially adopted Christianity and ordered all the Egyptian temples to close. It is at this point that ancient Egypt ends, having withstood everything but the loss of its gods.

THE RIVER OF LIFE

The one constant in five millennia of Egyptian history is the Nile River. The Greek historian Herodotus called Egypt "the gift of the Nile" and it is difficult to improve upon this description, since the country depends on the river for its very existence. Without the Nile—which runs through Egypt for only the last one-third of its course from the northeast corner of Africa to the Mediterranean—there would simply be desert, its closeness a constant reminder to

the Egyptians of their reliance upon the river. Before the building of modern dams, the Nile flooded every year, depositing rich black silt that produced an abundance of crops. This abundance was personified by the androgynous god Hapy, who is said to have caused "the meadows to laugh when the riverbanks are flooded," and was honored with hymns of joy. The strip of greenery bordering the river—in sharp contrast to the sand and rock beyond—is an age-old sight echoed in the horizontal layering often found in Egyptian art.

THE ART OF ANCIENT EGYPT

Ancient Egyptian art was mainly inspired by familiar images taken from nature. Its distinctive style was formalized at the very beginning of the historic period and remained largely unchanged for three thousand years. The often breathtaking beauty of most Egyptian paintings, relief, sculpture, and jewelry is secondary to its function, which was originally either religious or funerary, or both.

The majority of art was made to adorn the darkness of temple interiors, away from public view, or else to be buried with the dead in their tombs in order to protect and sustain them in the afterlife. This explains why two-dimensional scenes, with their apparently simplistic form and lack of perspective, can initially appear as almost childish to modern eyes. But this is to misunderstand their basic functional purpose, since it was believed that the correct ritual formulae could literally bring such representations to life. In order to be able to see, hear, smell, and speak as fully as possible, the image of a deity or of a deceased person had to be portrayed with every relevant physical feature depicted as clearly as possible. In art in two dimensions the face is therefore shown in profile to give maximum definition to the eyes and mouth, while the eye is represented whole, as if seen from the front.

RIGHT Fabulously crafted in gold, lapis lazuli, carnelian, and feldspar, this rearing *uraeus* (cobra) was made for King Senwosret II; it represents Wadjet, the snake goddess of Lower Egypt, who was set on the king's brow to spit fire into the eyes of his enemies.

FAR RIGHT A painted relief of the goddess Isis from the temple of King Sety I at Abydos. She wields a *sistrum*, a metal rattle used in sacred rites. For the Egyptians, to depict a ritual was, literally, to ensure its perpetual performance.

BELOW This painted plaster panel was found in the *mastaba* tomb of Neferma'at and Atet at Meidum, and dates from the early 4th dynasty. The geese are arranged symmetrically with a balance of stylization and naturalism that characterizes much of Egyptian art.

Inanimate objects would also be depicted as clearly as possible: items on a table were shown piled up in distinct layers, even to the point of appearing to float in air. The same was the case with the contents of a closed box—which in reality would have been hidden from view and thus effectively "lost" if portrayed realistically. The real food and drink placed in a temple or a tomb to sustain a deity or a dead person would also be depicted and described on the walls, and accompanying scenes and models of food production would ensure a constant supply of sustenance for eternity.

Even portrayals of physical activities, such as dancing, were created for a specific purpose, despite the fact that nowadays they are often popularly regarded as little more than pleasant decoration. However, the depiction of dance and the playing of lively music was believed to assist in awakening the god in its temple shrine or in reviving the senses of the deceased in his or her tomb.

COLOR AND SPIRIT

The functional, coded nature of Egyptian art was enhanced by the careful choice of material and color. The land of Egypt, represented politically by the White Crown of Upper Egypt and the Red Crown of Lower Egypt, was also divided into the "Black Land" (Kemet), where vegetation flourished, and the hostile red desert wastes (Deshret); hence, black and green were used in representations of Osiris (opposite), the god of fertility and eternal life, while red was used in depictions of his evil brother Seth, the god of chaos. The calm, ethereal blue of the sky, as reflected in the Nile, was echoed in the choice of blue to represent divinity, and the golden yellow of the sun was a protective hue. Men and women were conventionally depicted with different skin colors, as in the statue (above) of the priest Tenti and his wife Imeretef (ca. 2400 BCE): the ruddy shade used for males contrasts with the paler tones of females.

WORDS OF THE GODS

Ancient Egyptian art is inseparable from the script that accompanies it. These "picture words," known as hieroglyphs, from the Greek word for "sacred carved writing," first developed ca. 3100 BCE and were initially employed by a small literate bureaucracy to keep records. Later, the script came to be used for the monumental stone inscriptions covering tombs, temples, obelisks, and sculpture, as well as for ritual texts on papyrus and religious objects.

LEFT The ibis-headed Thoth (Djehuty), god of knowledge, was regarded as the inventor of hieroglyphic writing. The Egyptians believed that the sun god, Re, allowed Thoth to pass on the meaning of hieroglyphs to humans to enable them to organize and administer their country.

Because they mostly appeared in a religious context, hieroglyphs were known in Egyptian as *medou netjer*, "words of the gods." They were said to have been invented by Thoth, the god of writing. The cursive "shorthand" form of hieroglyphs, referred to as hieratic ("sacred script"), was employed for day-to-day transactions, and this was superseded in the Late Period by a widespread form called "demotic" ("popular script").

From this time use was increasingly made of Greek letters to write the Egyptian language, and in the Roman era a Greek-based alphabet—called Coptic from *Aiguptos*, the Greek word for "Egyptian"—became popular among a growing Christian population. Hieroglyphs remained in use by the priests of the old religion, but the Roman ban on non-Christian worship in 392 CE spelled the end of the ancient writing system. The last firmly dated hieroglyphic inscription was made at Philae on August 24, 394 CE. Knowledge of hieroglyphs died with the last priests of the old faith, and their meaning was lost for fourteen hundred years.

For centuries, people wrongly assumed that the strange ancient signs were entirely symbolic, and many wildly inaccurate attempts

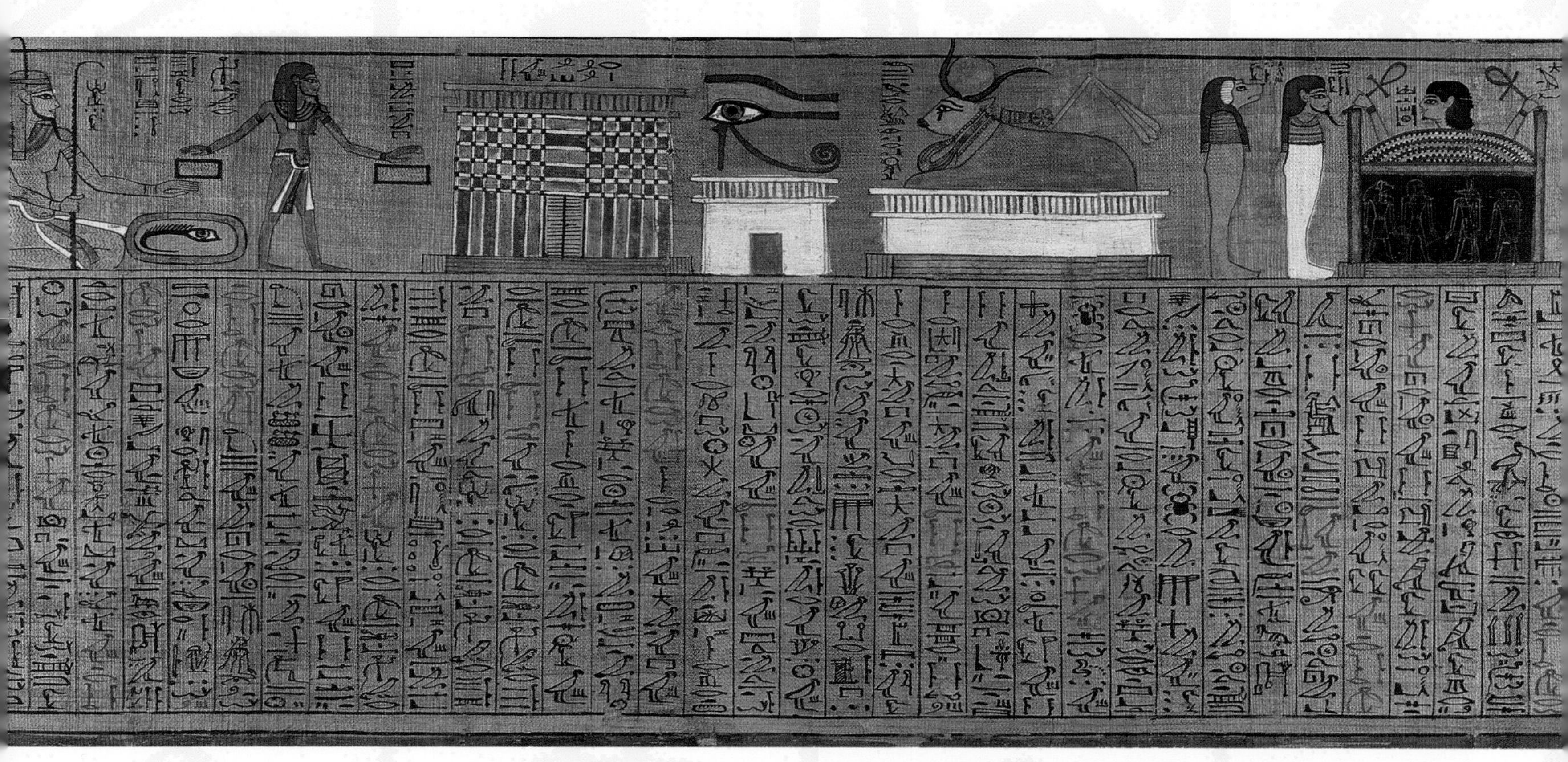

at translation were made. However, in 1799 an ancient inscription was discovered by French soldiers at el-Rashid (Rosetta) on the Mediterranean coast. It was a royal decree issued during the reign of King Ptolemy V (205–180 BCE), and it was written twice in Egyptian (in hieroglyphs and demotic) and once in Greek. By enabling linguists to compare the same text in Egyptian and a living tongue, Greek, the "Rosetta Stone" proved the key to unlocking the language—and through it, the civilization—of ancient Egypt for the modern world.

ABOVE In this page from the Book of the Dead of the 19th-dynasty royal scribe Ani, the text is written in hieratic, a cursive form of hieroglyphs. The illustrated border features a central *wedjat* (Eye of Horus, see page 70).

The Englishman Thomas Young (1773–1829) was the first to recognize that hieroglyphs could be phonetic, with signs representing individual sounds and not just whole words or concepts. But he did not appreciate the full implications of this discovery, and it was a Frenchman, Jean-François Champollion (1790–1832), who first revealed the great complexity of the Egyptian writing system. From his study of the Rosetta Stone, Champollion revealed that hieroglyphs consisted of three basic types of sign: "phonograms" (representing sounds), "ideograms" and "logograms" (representing whole words), and "determinatives" (which simply emphasize meaning). The phonograms in turn fall into three categories. There is a basic "alphabet" of twenty-four hieroglyphs, each of which represents a single consonant (for example, [hieroglyph] = b, [hieroglyph] = m, [hieroglyph] = r). Other phonograms—several hundred in total—are categorized as representing either two sounds or three sounds (for example, [hieroglyph] = ms, [hieroglyph] = nfr).

For most of Egyptian history, vowels were not written and where a vowel is not known, Egyptologists conventionally insert an "e" so that a word can be pronounced. Hieroglyphs can be written vertically (from top to bottom) or horizontally (from left to right or right to left). There is no punctuation.

The use of hieroglyphs was largely restricted to a literate elite who made up approximately 1 percent of the population, and although professional scribes were generally men, some women were also literate. Literacy was greatly valued as a means of social advancement, because scribes naturally formed the core personnel of Egypt's government and bureaucracy.

LEFT The black basalt slab known as the Rosetta Stone bears the same inscription in three scripts: hieroglyphs (top), demotic (middle), and Greek (bottom). By comparing the Egyptian to the Greek, 19th-century linguists were able to decipher the ancient Egyptian language. The stone dates from 196 BCE—the ninth year of the reign of Ptolemy V—and records the honors given to the king by the priests of Memphis.

The written word was believed to hold great power, comparable to that contained within artistic images, which explains the fact that some hieroglyphic symbols in religious inscriptions were occasionally mutilated as they were carved to "neutralize" potential dangers. Royal names were written within an oval ring, or "cartouche" ( ) to protect them, line upon line of cartouches making up the "King Lists" that record the royal lineage. These King Lists were often highly selective—those monarchs who were regarded as less than perfect by later pharaohs were deleted from the official records. If a royal name was removed in this way, or scraped or chiseled from his own monuments, it was as if the individual concerned had ceased to exist. This fate befell several pharaohs in the course of Egyptian history, including the "heretic" Akhenaten. Conversely, simply to speak the name of a deceased person was believed to make him or her live again, which explains why the name of the deceased is so frequently repeated in tomb inscriptions.

RIGHT The Abydos "King List," a section of which is shown here, comes from the 19th-dynasty temple of Ramesses II. The cartouches of the king's names alternate with those of his illustrious predecessors (although those rulers who were considered unworthy of inclusion—such as Hatshepsut and Akhenaten—were omitted from the official record).

Because of their potency, names were carefully chosen, and often included the name of a god or king—for example, Amenhotep ("Amun is Content"), Tutankhamun ("Living Image of Amun"), and Pepiankh ("Pepi Lives"). Simpler names included Nefer ("Beautiful," as in Nefertiti and Nefertari), Seneb ("Healthy"), and Sheshen ("Lotus"), which became—via Hebrew—the name Susannah or Susan.

RA = (SUN GOD) + MES (CHILD) + SSU (REED) = RAMESSES

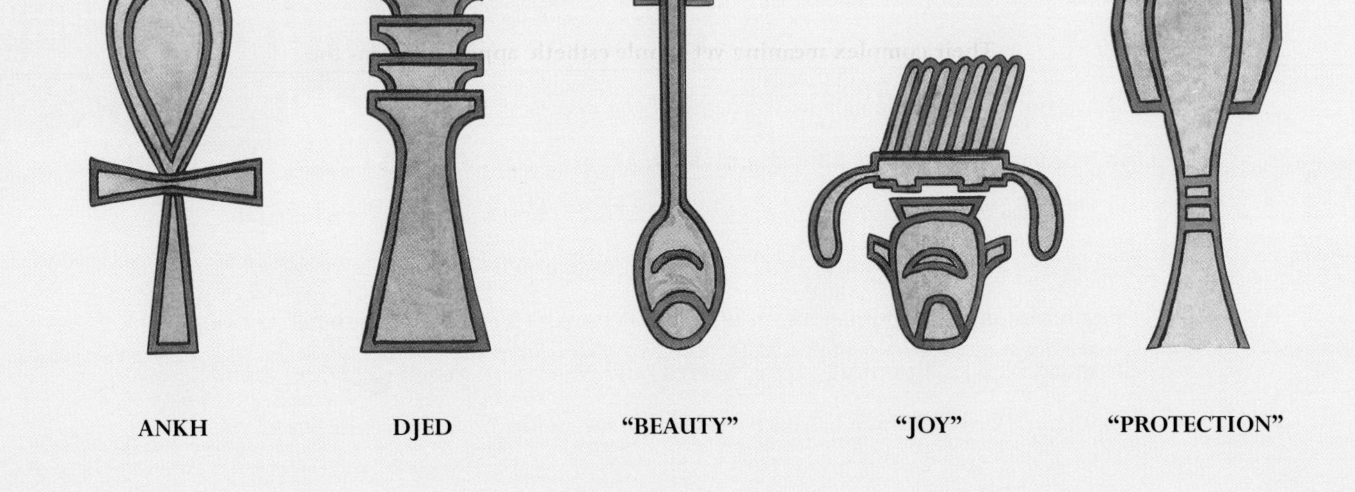

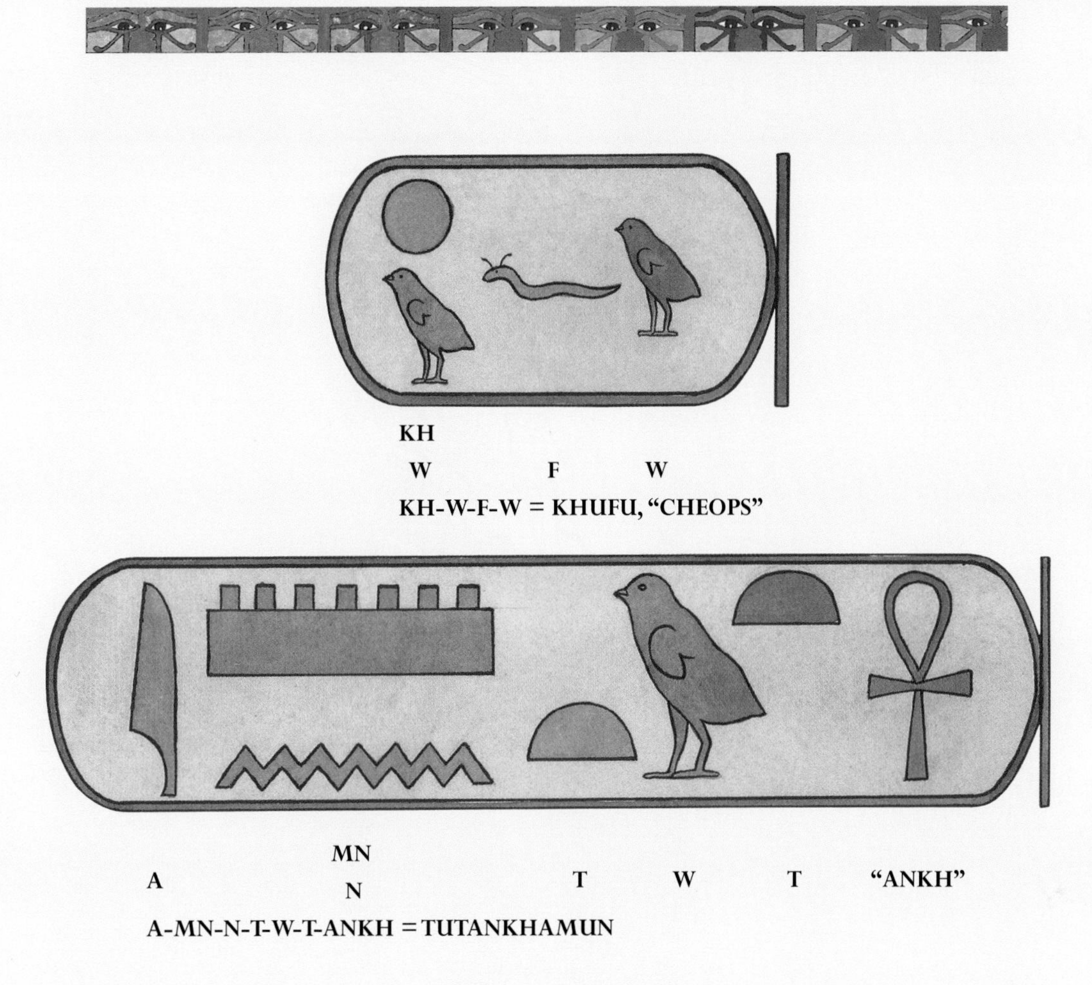

GLYPH AND SYMBOL

Their complex meaning yet simple esthetic appeal explains the use of hieroglyphs as both a functional and decorative device. They appeared in all aspects of Egyptian life, from great stone edifices to small items of personal jewelry. For example, the *djed* symbol, representing the backbone of Osiris, meant stability and strength. The "key of life" sign, or *ankh*, was another frequently used symbol, alongside the signs for beauty, joy, and protection, among others, and the potent names of gods and kings. Royal names were written in an oval ring, or cartouche, and if they contained the name of a god, this was always placed first. Thus Tutankhamun ("Living Image of Amun") was written "Amun-Tut-Ankh."

SYMBOLS IN STONE
Nowhere is the effect of the hieroglyphic script felt more powerfully than in the monumental inscriptions that cover the Egyptians' vast religious and funerary buildings. The ever-changing play of sunlight and shadow creates a constantly shifting image throughout the course of the day, but the lines of pictorial script and accompanying artistic scenes convey an overall feeling of balance. This can be seen particularly at Karnak, from the sublime raised reliefs of its Middle

Kingdom chapels to the sunken relief of the repetitious cartouches of the Ramesside pharaohs of the New Kingdom (above). The Ramesside kings carved their royal names and titles deeply into the stone, in the hope that they would last for eternity. Should the name be erased, as happened with "anomalous" rulers such as Akhenaten and Hatshepsut in the 18th dynasty, the individual would be consigned to oblivion—which for the Egyptians was the most terrible fate imaginable.

THE SEDGE AND THE BEE

LEFT The two granite pillars that adorn the Hall of Records of Thutmose III at the Karnak temple are carved in the forms of the papyrus and lotus, the heraldic plants of Upper and Lower Egypt, symbolizing the unity of the two lands.

RIGHT This scene from the 18th-dynasty Theban tomb of the royal scribe Nebamun shows the tomb owner hunting in the papyrus marshes, accompanied by his wife (a priestess) and their daughter. Nebamun is portrayed actively restoring order to a scene of disorder, represented by the flapping of the birds' wings.

The dual world of ancient Egypt—river and desert, fertile strip and barren wastes, land of the Sedge (Upper Egypt) and land of the Bee (Lower Egypt)—was held in balance by the gods, through their intermediary, the king. He was supported by the priesthood, the nobility, and the civil service, who in turn depended on the producers of Egypt's economic wealth. Most of the population lived on the land, and the afterlife was conceived as an idyllic, eternally prosperous agrarian landscape, in which the dead were depicted plowing, sowing, reaping, and hunting.

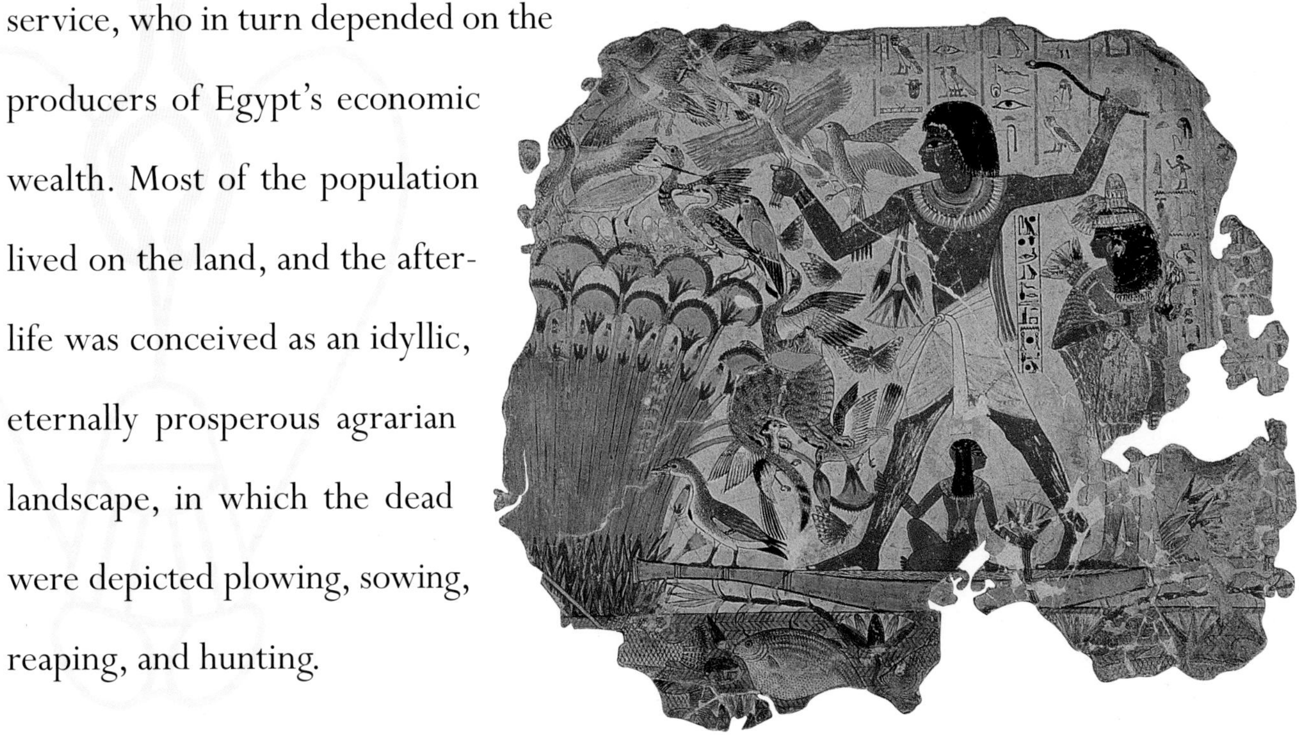

BOUNTIES OF THE BLACK LAND

BELOW This statue dates from ca. 2500 BCE and was discovered in a tomb at Sakkara. It depicts the deceased as a scribe seated in the classic pose of his profession, with a papyrus scroll open on his lap and his pen poised. His rather pendulous breasts and incipient paunch are also typical of scribal portraits and indicate a well-fed—and therefore prosperous—individual.

The Egyptians imagined a universe created and regulated by the gods, a place of balance, truth, and harmony—characteristics personified by the goddess Ma'at. They conceived of the afterlife simply as a parallel Egypt, complete with its dominating river, where there was neither illness nor famine, a place where crops grew to a great height free of drought or insect damage, and where harvesting was an easy task to be performed in one's finery.

In reality, the rich bounty provided by the Nile did not come without hard work on the part of the farmers who grew the country's staple crops of barley and wheat. They broadcast seed by hand in the fall, following the Nile's annual summer flood, which watered the fields and replenished them with deposits of rich black silt. To take full advantage of the inundation, and to increase the amount of farmland available, farmers also undertook widespread irrigation schemes.

RIGHT In this detail from the New Kingdom tomb of Sennedjem, the deceased and his wife are depicted harvesting in the afterlife, dressed in their finest clothes. In life, however, work on the land—undertaken by the majority population of farmers and manual workers—was dirty and laborious.

Although the majority of the ancient population was involved in agriculture and food production, many people were also potters, weavers, carpenters, metalworkers, and stonemasons—the craftspeople responsible for the buildings and artifacts so greatly admired today. But the most privileged occupation of all was that of the scribe, a position exempt from taxation and carrying considerable prestige and authority, to the extent that officials often chose to be portrayed as a scribe, cross-legged with a papyrus scroll unrolled on his lap, reed pen in hand, and perhaps an ink palette slung over one shoulder.

Scribes were trained in schools attached to temples, and mastering the complexities of hieroglyphic writing was a long and arduous task. In the text known as *The*

Satire of the Trades, a father encourages his son in his studies to become a scribe, "the greatest of all callings." After ridiculing the hardships of other professions—"each more wretched than the other"—the father concludes that "there's no profession without a boss, except for the scribe; he is the boss. Hence if you know writing it will be better for you than any other profession."

The small, unfinished tomb of Neferherenptah, known as the "Bird Tomb," takes its name from the various agricultural scenes—including bird hunting—that decorate its walls. The tomb is located at Sakkara and dates from the 5th dynasty (ca. 2315 BCE).

ART AND NATURE

Ancient Egyptian craftsmen were very much inspired by the natural world around them. Working within strict artistic conventions, they yet succeeded in capturing the vitality of familiar plants, animals, and birds, and in giving them a functional purpose. The images chosen repeatedly emphasize the concept of regeneration and were believed to have the ability to transmit the very life force that they represented—from the scarab beetle and tilapia fish, which were believed capable of self-generation, to the animals and plants offered as food to the souls of the dead. Geese, depicted in a famous painted frieze from Meidum (see pages 14–15), were symbols of the earth god Geb and also of Amun. The life-giving properties of the Nile were represented by the papyrus reed and lotus flower, the heraldic symbols respectively of Upper and Lower Egypt.

ABOVE **This wood statue, covered with painted plaster, from the tomb of Meketre at Thebes, ca. 2000 BCE, depicts a female servant bringing offerings.**

ROLES AND IMAGES

In the early days of Egyptology, European gentlemen-scholars were startled to discover images of Egyptian women in prominent or even dominating roles. They dismissed much of what they found as "fictional" or "ritualistic," and even today the issue of equality is controversial. But in ancient Egypt women were legally independent citizens and they exercised varying degrees of self-determination unusual in the male-dominated ancient world. Their freedom certainly shocked the Greeks: the historian Herodotus (5th century BCE) wrote that women "go to market and take part in trading, whereas men sit at home and do the weaving." The Egyptians, he concluded, "seem to have reversed the normal practices of mankind."

RIGHT **Female servants wait on the wealthy in this banquet scene from the 18th-dynasty tomb of Rekhmire in Thebes. As the central servant girl—unusually shown from the back rather than the side—pours out perfume for the seated lady on her right, she says: "For your *ka* (soul)."**

Generally, women married and had children, but nevertheless they were visible throughout Egyptian society, laboring in the fields and conscripted alongside men for public works. Both male and female servants are portrayed cleaning houses, making beds, brewing, and baking—although laundry was done by professional washermen. As for their wealthy employers, the men usually worked outside the home whereas women, although shown in outdoor scenes, spent considerably more of their time indoors—as reflected in the artistic convention that generally gives them paler skin. But both men and women attended social occasions together.

Women were paid for the work they did, and could own, buy, and sell their own property, make wills, and choose which of their children would inherit. Many women held religious posts and females are also known to have held the titles of "governor," "judge," "steward," "overseer of doctors," and even "vizier"—the highest administrative rank below the king. The monarch was generally male, but women occupied the throne in their own right on at least five occasions.

Although it is often stated that there is no evidence of female scribes, some women must have been able to consult written records in the course of their official

duties. By Greco-Roman times women's literacy is well proven: the famous Cleopatra VII wrote and spoke at least seven languages, including Egyptian—she was the first of the Ptolemaic dynasty to learn the language of her subjects.

The tendency to avoid sexual stereotyping applied also to deities. Gods and goddesses might be either passive or active, and many of Egypt's most fearsome deities were female (see pages 58–61). The potential for female aggression is reflected in texts and in depictions of women stabbing soldiers, firing arrows, and physically overpowering men—images supported by the weapons found with female burials.

FASHION AND FINERY

With their fine linen clothing, elaborately styled coiffures, colorful jewelry, and striking cosmetics, the Egyptians were an extremely image-conscious people. Appearances were of paramount importance and their style of dress developed from a sense of practicality combined with a love of beauty. Clothing was designed to counteract the effects of the climate. Most garments were simply constructed from plain linen, the basic Egyptian wardrobe consisting of a kilt (often with tunic and cloak) for men and a dress for women, together with a loincloth and sandals for both sexes. This relatively simple clothing was generally offset by collars, necklaces, bracelets, anklets, belts, and earrings. The effect was completed—by both men and women—with the addition of a wig or false braids, black or green eyepaint, and a generous amount of perfume.

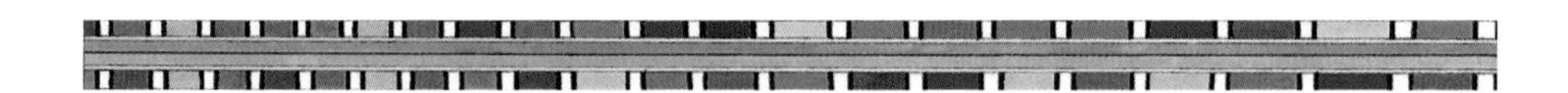

THE CELESTIAL WORLD

LEFT Carved on the ceiling of the Ptolemaic-period temple of the goddess Hathor at Dendera, the so-called "Dendera Zodiac" depicts the deities and celestial beings believed to inhabit the Egyptian heavens (see pages 108–109). The original ceiling is now displayed in the Musée du Louvre in Paris, France.

RIGHT This scene, also from Dendera, portrays the arched body of the sky goddess Nut. She is shown swallowing the sun as it begins its nighttime journey through her body; she then gives birth to it each dawn so that it can illuminate the land—here shown in stylized form with, in the center, an image bearing the face of Hathor that represents Dendera temple.

Egyptian religion was highly complex and involved the worship of the many gods and goddesses whose painted, incised, and sculpted images can still be seen today adorning tombs and temples and a great range of everyday artifacts. It was above all, except during the Amarna period (see page 50), a tolerant, all-encompassing belief system, which was able to embrace apparently contradictory myths and legends. Every story about the gods had its local variations, but each was regarded as no less valid than the next. Even such a fundamental myth as the story of the creation of the world came in three strikingly different—but equally accepted—versions.

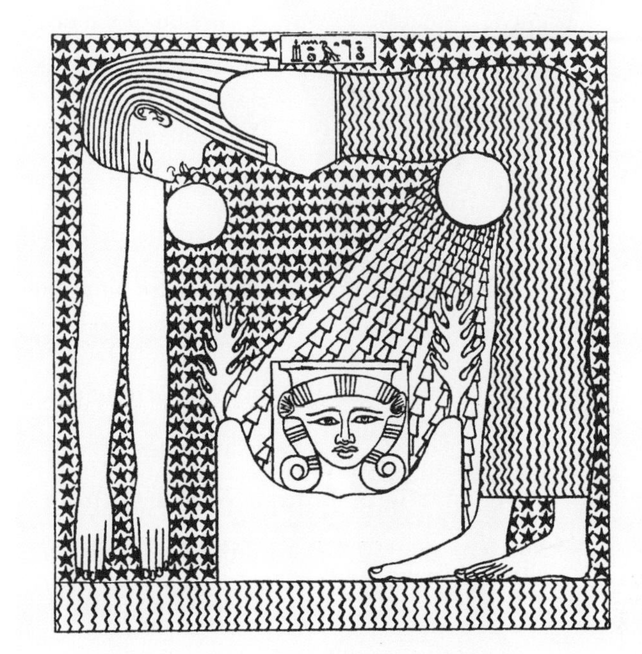

THE MANY FROM THE ONE

The Egyptians believed that life first emerged from the dark and formless void of Nun, the waters of chaos. At the beginning of time, a mound of earth rose out of Nun—an event that was graphically reenacted every year when the land began to appear above the receding floodwaters of the Nile—and it was on this mound that the gods created life.

The important Egyptian temples of Heliopolis, Hermopolis, and Memphis each claimed to mark the site of the primeval mound. At Heliopolis, the supreme creator was considered to be the sun god Atum, who emerged as the first sunrise from a lotus flower that sprouted on the mound. Atum contained within himself the life force of the universe, from which he created the twin gods Shu, the god of air, and Tefnut, the goddess of moisture. Atum did this either by ejaculating or, according to another version of the myth, by "sneezing out Shu and spitting out Tefnut."

Shu and Tefnut coupled to produce the earth god Geb and the sky goddess Nut, who had intercourse together. Shu separated them, but not before they had produced four children: Osiris, Isis, Seth, and Nephthys. Thereafter, Shu supported the arched body of Nut, which formed the sky and held back the forces of chaos. These nine gods are known as the Ennead (from Greek *ennea*, "nine").

The Memphis account of creation was based on the creative word of the god Ptah, who personified the primeval mound. Ptah thought the world into being and made all things a reality simply by speaking their names. One theory holds that the name of a shrine to Ptah at Memphis, Hwt-ka-Ptah, became *Aiguptos*, the Greek word that is the origin of "Egypt."

According to the priests of Hermopolis, the first life was formed by the eight deities of the Ogdoad (Greek *okto*, "eight"), who existed in the primeval waters.

LEFT Ptah, the creator god of Memphis who created the entire universe simply by using the power of his mind, is generally depicted as a modestly clad, bare-headed figure holding a *was* (scepter), as in this Late Period statue.

RIGHT The Hermopolis account of creation is depicted in this scene from the Book of the Dead of the priest Khensumose (ca. 1000 BCE). On the first day of creation, the sun rises in three stages over the primeval mound, which is surrounded by waters poured out by two female deities associated with the north (right) and the south (left). On the mound are eight figures representing the Ogdoad creator deities, who are depicted tilling the soil of the first land.

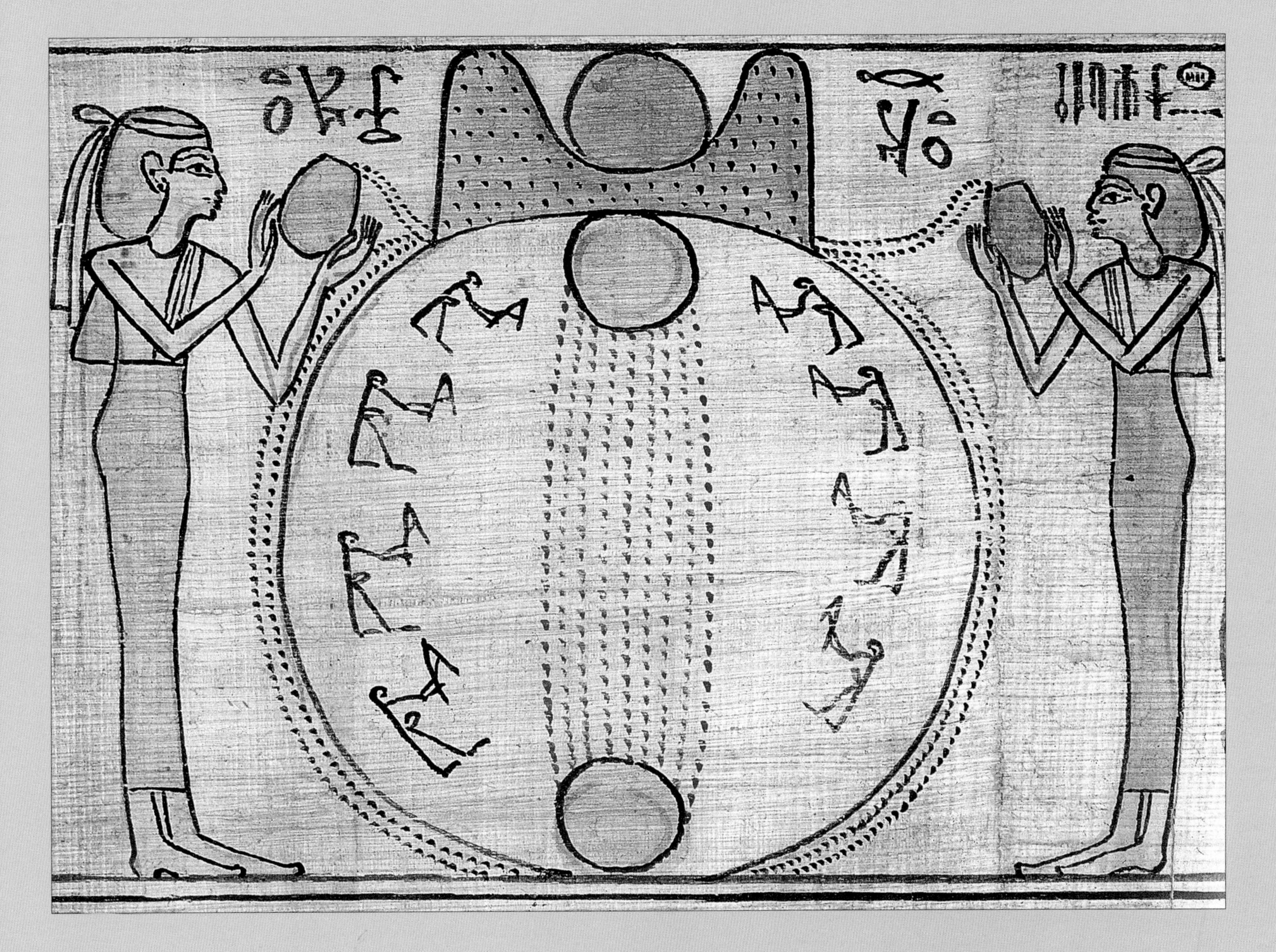

Nun and his female counterpart, Naunet, represented the forces of the waters themselves; Heh and Hauhet represented infinity; Kek and Kauket represented darkness; and Amun and Amaunet represented the hidden force of life. From the combined energy of the Ogdoad, life sprang into being and the primeval mound was created, from which the sun burst forth.

THE LORD OF THE HORIZON

The sun has always been the dominant factor in Egyptian life. It is both creator and destroyer, responsible for the barren desert and the rich harvests of the floodplain. In ancient Egypt, the sun was the supreme divinity, although both the sun and sun god came in many guises. As the universal source of energy, the sun's light brought order to the chaos of darkness, and as the first dawn broke over the primeval mound (see page 38), so life began. The cult center of the sun was Iunu, better known by its Greek name of Heliopolis ("City of the Sun"), where the myth of the Ennead taught that the creative power of the sun, in the form of the god Atum ("the All"), made all things (see page 38). By contrast, in other versions of the creation myth, the sun itself was created along with everything else in the universe.

LEFT **A single granite obelisk carved with the cartouches of Ramesses II (ca. 1279–1213 BCE) marks the gateway to the temple of Luxor (the matching second obelisk that once stood at the other side of the entrance now stands in the Place de la Concorde in Paris, France). Obelisks, the tips of which were once embellished with gold, were constructed to represent the primeval mound from which the sun first arose at the beginning of creation.**

The sun god generally took the form of the god Re, or Ra, whose name simply means "the Sun." Re is depicted as a falcon, a ram, or a human with a falcon's or ram's head. The god's form changed with the sun's daily passage through the sky. At dawn, the sun was Khepri ("the Evolving One"), represented by the scarab. As this beetle pushes along a ball of dung, so Khepri was imagined propelling the sun through the sky. The sun rising in the east was associated, too, with the falcon god Horus ("the Far One"), also known as Harakhty ("Horus of the Horizon"). The two were often combined as a single solar deity, Re-Harakhty.

RIGHT **On this painted wooden funerary stela the lady Taperet (ca. 900 BCE) is shown praying to the falcon-headed sun god Re-Harakhty before a table laden with offerings of bread, wine, and lotus flowers. In return the god, equipped with symbols representing power, radiates his beneficial solar rays toward her.**

Similarly, Re was again associated with Atum, in the form of Re-Atum, to represent the sun at the end of the day. As the sun set in the west, to be swallowed by the sky goddess Nut, it sank down into the underworld (Duat). On his nocturnal journey through the underworld, Re confronted the forces of darkness and chaos, led by his eternal enemy Apep, or Apophis, the giant serpent of chaos. Apep nightly threatened to swallow the sun and so destroy all life. Each dawn, after Apep had been subdued, Re emerged victorious from the underworld, reborn in the east as the child of Nut amid the redness of her birth blood (see page 37).

This pectoral, which is made of gold and semiprecious stones, represents Khepri—the rising sun—with the sun disk. The pectoral was discovered in the tomb of Tutankhamun (ca. 1332–1322 BCE) in the Valley of the Kings, western Thebes.

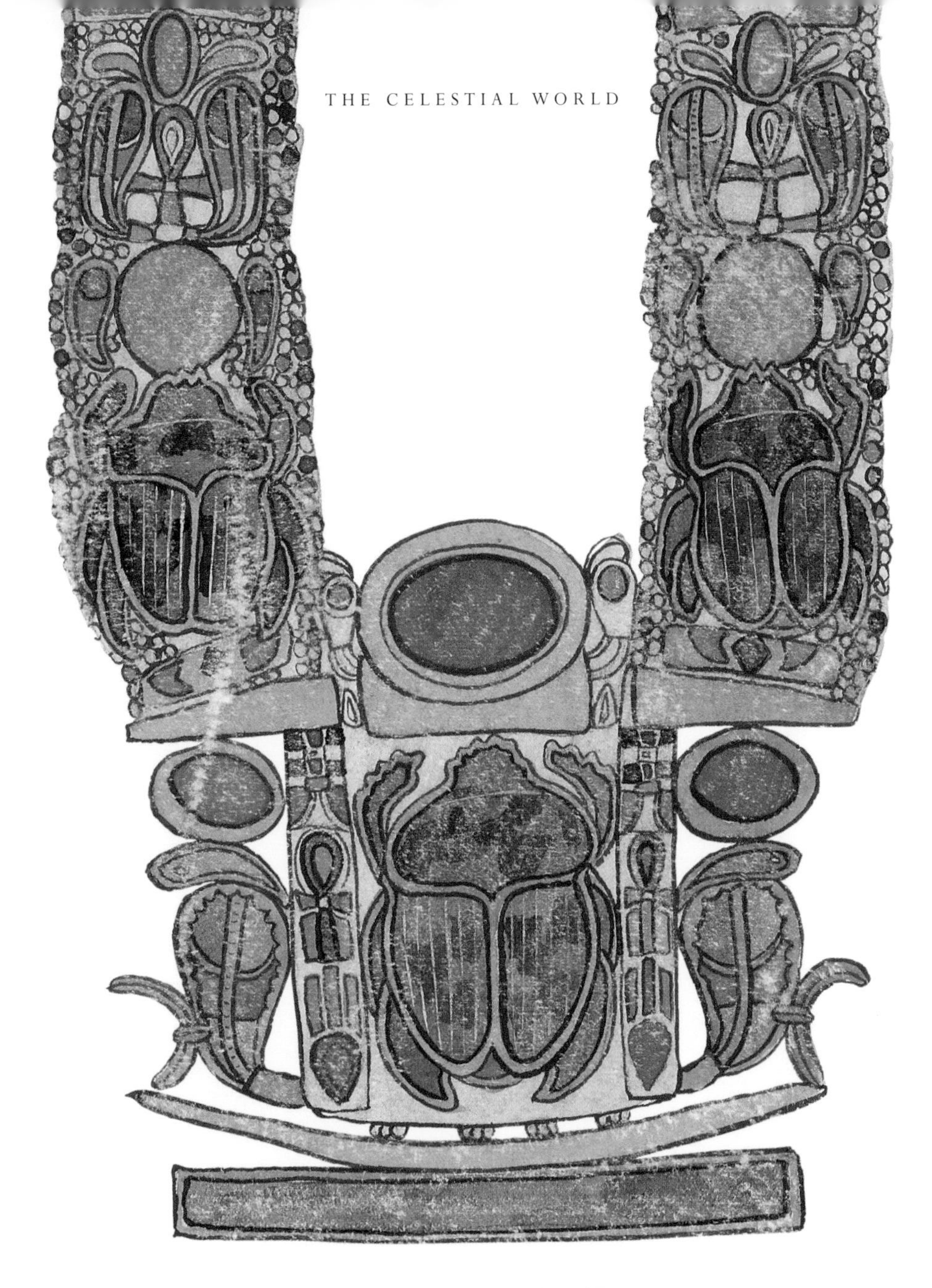

THE SACRED SCARAB

The scarab, or dung beetle, represented Khepri, the sun at dawn. The god's name means "the Evolving One"—the Egyptians believed the scarab to be self-generating, because its young emerged as if from nowhere from the ball of dung in which they were incubated. As the parent beetle was often seen rolling a dung ball (above, left), so, too, Khepri was depicted pushing up the sun. The young scarab crawled from its ball and took flight—an act believed to represent the sun god rising up into the heavens. A potent symbol of rebirth, the scarab features prominently in funerary art, as in the exquisite pectoral jewelry that adorns royal mummies.

SEATS OF RE: THE PYRAMIDS

The sun god came into being on the primeval mound of creation (see page 39). This mound was said to be represented by the structures that are without doubt ancient Egypt's most familiar monuments: the pyramids. The three great pyramids at Giza are the most famous examples, but more than eighty pyramids of varying size were built between the 3rd and 12th dynasties, the best surviving pyramids dating from the Old Kingdom (3rd to 5th dynasties, 2675–2350 BCE)—all of them sited within a 12-mile (20-kilometer) radius of the ancient capital, Memphis. The earliest pyramid is the 3rd-dynasty "step pyramid" of Sakkara, so called because of its step-like structure, which evolved from the earlier rectangular tomb known from its appearance as a *mastaba* (Arabic, "bench").

Constructed by the architect Imhotep as a tomb for his king, Djoser, or Zoser (ca. 2650 BCE), the step pyramid began as a

RIGHT The pyramids at Giza. Farthest from the camera—but the largest of the group at 479 feet (146 m) high—is the Great Pyramid of Khufu (Cheops). In the center is the 470-foot (143.5-m) pyramid of Khafre (Chephren). The smallest of the three, built by Menkaure (Mycerinus), stands a mere 215 feet (65.5 m) high.

mastaba before being raised to a height of 200 feet (60 meters) by adding four further, and successively smaller, *mastabas* to produce its stepped profile.

The transition from the step pyramid to the true pyramid is attributed to King Snofru (ca. 2625–2585 BCE), the first ruler of the 4th dynasty. The partial collapse of Snofru's pyramid at Meidum reveals how its original stepped sides were filled in to create a smooth outline. Snofru's "Bent Pyramid" at Dahshur was probably the first monument planned from the outset as a true pyramid, but his architects changed the gradient of its sides part of the way up, probably because the original angle was found to be too unstable. In the end, the first true pyramid was to be Snofru's "Red Pyramid," again at Dahshur.

Once the technique of building a true pyramid had been perfected, it was duplicated at Giza by Snofru's son Khufu (Cheops), who created the "Great Pyramid," the largest pyramid of all. Nearby lies the pyramid of Khufu's son, Khafre (Chephren), whose pyramid and associated

LEFT The only known portrait of Khufu (ca. 2585–2560 BCE), the builder of the Great Pyramid, is this tiny ivory statuette, which is just 3 inches (8 cm) tall. The statuette was found in two pieces—head and body—at Abydos in 1903.

RIGHT The step pyramid of King Djoser was constructed ca. 2650 BCE by the king's architect Imhotep in a series of ascending bench-shape *mastaba* structures. A number of subsidiary buildings, originally surrounded by a vast enclosure wall, stand alongside the pyramid.

temple structures—including the Sphinx (see page 80)—form the most complete of all such funerary complexes. The smaller pyramid of Khafre's son, Menkaure (Mycerinus), completes the monuments of the Giza plateau.

The 5th-dynasty pyramids at Abusir and Sakkara are much smaller and, rather than being made of solid stone, consist of stone facings on a core of rubble. The pyramid of Unas (ca. 2371–2350 BCE) was the first to include any kind of inscription. The interior walls of his pyramid, like those of his 6th-dynasty successors, are inscribed with funerary writings known as the "Pyramid Texts."

Following the Old Kingdom's decline, pyramid-building ceased. It began again at Dahshur, Lahun, and Hawara as the Middle Kingdom pharaohs reestablished their power. These pyramids had mudbrick cores and, when their outer stone casings were later stripped away, they eroded to formless stumps.

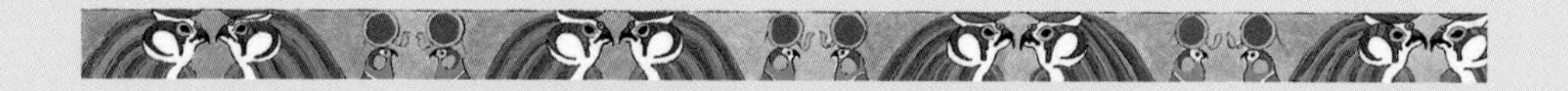

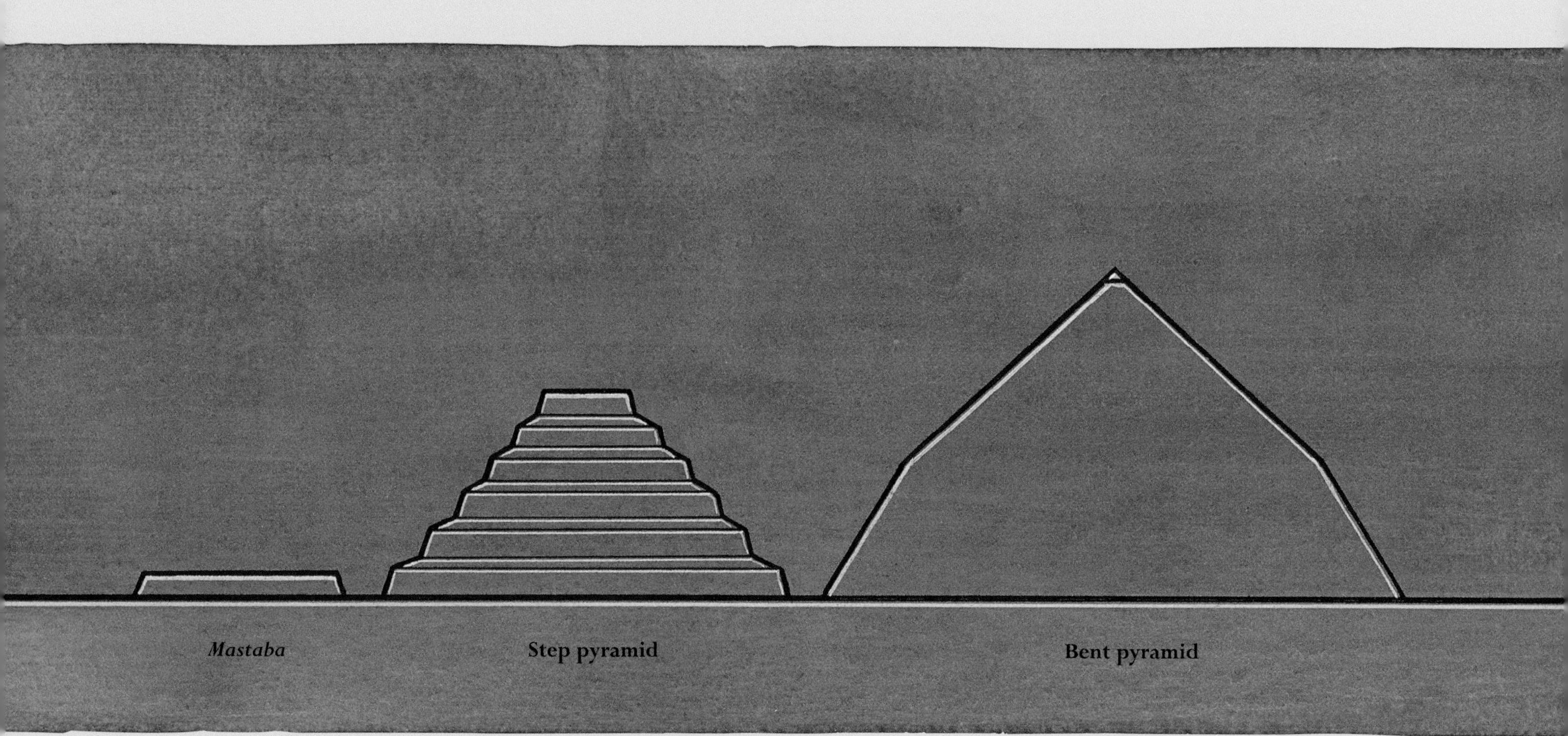

BIRTHPLACE OF THE SUN: PYRAMID FORMS

The pyramid structure developed from a simple mound over a body buried in the sand, which was believed to represent the primeval mound of creation on which the sun god was born (see page 39). The mound had taken on a more formal bench shape (*mastaba*) by the early dynastic period, from which the famous "steps" of Egypt's first pyramid were derived. Experiments with gradients followed, resulting

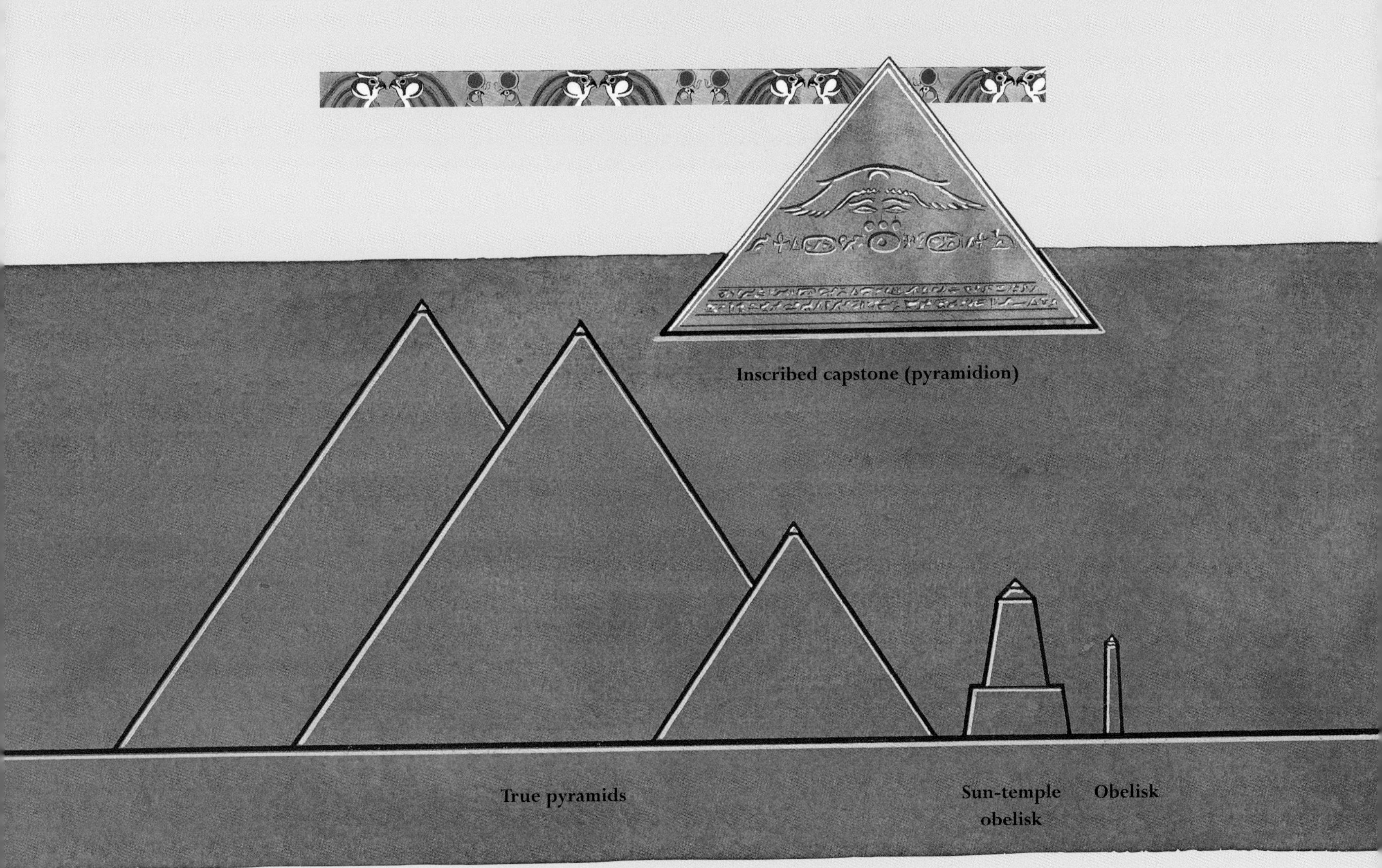

in the "bent" pyramid and later the first true pyramid. Every pyramid was topped with a small capstone, or pyramidion, that was often inscribed and gilded to reflect the sun's dawn rays. Fifth-dynasty kings built sun temples at Abusir centered on squat pyramid-like monuments. These were prototypes of later obelisks—tall, slender monoliths with pointed, gilded tips, also erected in honor of the sun.

THE HERETIC OF AMARNA

Although the sun remained the supreme deity throughout Egyptian history, the Theban pharaohs of the early New Kingdom elevated their local god, Amun, to the status of national deity, linking him with the sun god to create Amun-Re (see page 53). With the accession of Thutmose IV (ca. 1400–1390 BCE), whose claim to the throne was supported by the rival priests of the sun god in Heliopolis, political power began to shift away from Amun. The sun god was increasingly worshiped in the form of the Aten, the sun disk. Thutmose's son Amenhotep III (ca. 1390–1353 BCE), developed this policy further and restored the sun-centered kingship that had characterized the Pyramid Age a thousand years earlier.

LEFT Portrayals of King Amenhotep III, such as this huge head in red granite found at the site of the pharaoh's funerary temple in western Thebes, reveal his characteristic features of large, almond-shaped eyes, small nose, and smiling mouth. Amenhotep III is often shown as youthful and plump, representing the creative powers of the sun coupled with the fertility of the land and the inundation of the Nile. He eventually came to be depicted in a deified state as "the Sun God's Living Image on Earth."

Amenhotep III aligned himself with the sun god by taking the titles "Chosen One of Re," "Image of Re," and "the Dazzling Aten." The Aten name was also used for a royal barge, a battalion of soldiers, and a new royal palace on the west bank of the Nile at Thebes—deliberately distancing the king from the clergy of Amun, who were based at Karnak on the east bank.

The reign of Amenhotep's son Amenhotep IV, or Akhenaten (ca. 1353–1336 BCE), is usually described as a time of sudden change in Egyptian religion, art, and literature. These changes—the prominence given to the Aten, innovation in architecture, and the development of more naturalistic art styles—can actually be traced back to Amenhotep III. But they were taken further by Akhenaten. His zealous promotion of the Aten—or rather, of his father united with the sun in the form of the Aten—at the expense of Amun and the other gods and goddesses created widespread political and economic instability. Traditional temples were closed down and the capital was moved to a new city, Akhetaten (el-Amarna), which

RIGHT **Akhenaten is shown worshiping the light of the Aten (the sun disk) in this relief from an altar. The figures—Akhenaten's queen, Nefertiti, appears in the bottom left-hand corner—display the "elongated" style that characterized the "Amarna period," named after Akhenaten's new capital city at el-Amarna.**

Akhenaten ordered to be constructed in an isolated area of central Egypt.

In the confused aftermath of Akhenaten's reign, his ephemeral successors (who included his son Tutankhamun) restored order by returning to Thebes and reverting to the worship of the traditional gods led by Amun. The Aten—and Akhenaten himself, who was known from that time as "the Heretic of Amarna"—was simply obliterated from all official records.

THE UNKNOWABLE LORD

As one of the eight creator deities of the Ogdoad—"the fathers and mothers who were before the original gods" (see page 38)—Amun ("the Hidden One") appears in Egyptian creation mythology alongside his female equivalent, Amaunet, to represent the hidden life force of the universe. Amun was first mentioned in the 5th-dynasty pyramid inscriptions at Sakkara, in the north of the country, but it was in the south that he rose to prominence. He was worshiped as the local deity of the Theban region from at least as early as the 11th dynasty (ca. 2081–1938 BCE), and his fortunes rose with those of the Middle Kingdom pharaohs who originated from this area. Amun soon became known as "the King of the Gods."

LEFT **This small, painted limestone stela dates to ca. 1200 BCE. It was dedicated to the god Amun by the tomb's owner, Bai, and was found in the small temple of Hathor at Deir el-Medina. Amun is represented by his sacred animal, the ram (top). In the scene below (left), which is entitled "Adoration of Amun-Re by his servant Bai," the latter kneels to recite prayers addressed to the "Listening Ears" of the god, which are painted in the auspicious colors of black, yellow, and green (right).**

The center of the worship of Amun, at Karnak (on the east bank of the Nile at Thebes), was embellished by successive pharaohs until it became the largest temple complex in Egypt. As pharaohs offered increasing amounts of tribute to Karnak, Amun's priests began to accumulate wealth and power to rival that of the monarchy itself.

At Karnak, Amun was associated with the Theban goddess Mut, who was revered as one of the symbolic divine mothers of the pharaoh. She supplanted Amaunet as the consort of Amun. With their child, the moon god Khonsu, they made up the "Divine Triad." All three had temple complexes at Karnak.

Amun is generally depicted in human form wearing a distinctive double-plumed crown, but he can also be represented by a ram, a goose, or even a snake, the creatures that were sacred to him. As Amun-Kematef ("He Who Has Completed His

Moment"), he was envisioned as a snake shedding its skin in a constant cycle of renewal. Amun's creative power was reinforced when he was linked with the fertility god, Min, to create the ithyphallic Amun-Kamutef ("Bull of His Mother").

During the New Kingdom, Amun's status was further enhanced by linking him with the sun god, Egypt's supreme deity, to create Amun-Re, the ruler of the gods and—except during the Amarna Period (see page 50)—the state deity.

Ultimately, all Egypt's gods and goddesses came to be seen as aspects of Amun, who was believed to be the supreme mystery, the divine creative force of the universe. As such, he was referred to as "the Unknowable."

Amun also enjoyed genuine widespread popularity outside his great temple. He was worshiped in household shrines and addressed in the daily prayers of the people.

LEFT **Amun-Re is portrayed in this solid-gold cult statue from Thebes (possibly from the Karnak temple). The statue stands 7 inches (17.5 cm) high. Although the original plumes from the crown are lost, the god still holds a sickle sword, which points to a date sometime during the 22nd dynasty (ca. 945–712 BCE).**

THE DOMAIN OF AMUN

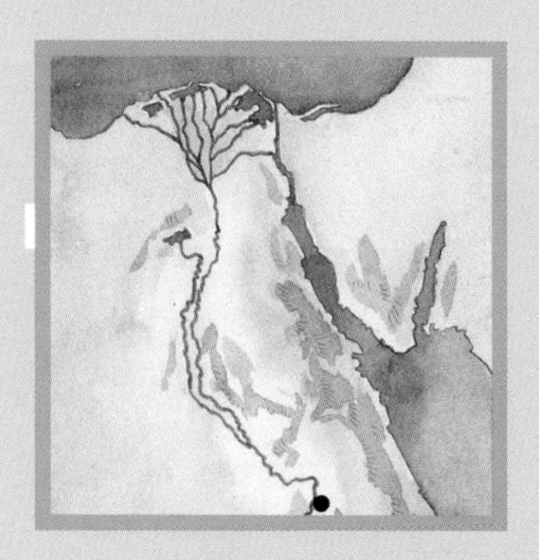

The origins of the great temple of Amun at Karnak date back to ca. 2000 BCE, when local rulers set up a shrine to the god. From that time on, almost all the pharaohs sought to display their piety by making additions to the temple, attempting in the process to outdo their predecessor in the size and splendor of the columns, pylons (ceremonial gateways), and statues erected in Amun's honor.

The temple itself was built along traditional Egyptian lines. It was constructed around a "holy of holies"—the innermost sanctuary in which Amun's cult statue resided, originally within a cedarwood shrine. This statue was thought capable of receiving the divine spirit of the god. The main temple axis runs westward from the sanctuary toward the Nile, with a second axis running south toward the separate temple of Amun's consort Mut. Set along each axis are hypostyle (columned) chambers, adorned with relief scenes of the pharaoh before the Divine

A general view of the temple complex of Amun at Karnak on the Theban east bank, showing the central Hypostyle Hall and obelisks, and looking west toward the Theban Hills and the famous Valley of the Kings beyond.

Triad of Amun, Mut, and their child Khonsu. The famous Hypostyle Hall built by Sety I (ca. 1290–1279 BCE) contains 134 huge columns, each carved in the form of a papyrus plant to create a magnificent stylized papyrus grove.

Before each of Karnak's columned halls stands a huge pylon that originally marked the front of the temple. The pylon was adorned with royal statuary, obelisks, and tall flagpoles that stood in the long vertical niches that can still be seen

LEFT **The now roofless Hypostyle Hall of Karnak temple covers an area of almost 6,000 square yards (5,000 sq m). Its 134 monumental columns set in sixteen rows are inscribed with the repeated cartouches of Ramesses II. However, the building work was undertaken by his father, Sety I, using plans drawn up by his own father, Ramesses I, first king of the 19th dynasty.**

on the façade. Successive pharaohs simply built their own halls and pylons in front of the existing ones, so the latest structures are farthest away from the central shrine—which was itself renewed by Philip Arrhidaeus (323–317 BCE). The pylon nearest the river is known as the First Pylon, but it dates from the late 30th dynasty and is therefore actually the last of Karnak's fourteen gateways to be built.

In front of the First Pylon is a processional avenue of ram-headed sphinxes, which once led to a small harbor linked to the Nile. This was the mooring place for the barque in which the cult statue of Amun was ferried either across the river to "visit" the royal funerary temples on the west bank, or upriver to the temple of Luxor just under two miles (2.9 kilometers) to the south. The god could also make the journey to Luxor overland, along another grand avenue of sphinxes.

BELOW **Ram-headed sphinxes sacred to Amun and carved with the cartouche of the 21st-dynasty king Psusennes I line the processional way leading from the first pylon of Karnak temple to the ceremonial quay-side on the river. A similar processional way of human-headed sphinxes links Karnak with the smaller Luxor temple to the southwest.**

THE MIGHTY GODDESSES

For the ancient Egyptians, every aspect of life combined elements that were both male and female, active and passive, aggressive and benign. In some lands, "female" might imply passive and gentle, but this was not the case in Egypt, as can clearly be seen in the way Egyptians perceived their gods and goddesses. In contrast to almost every other ancient culture, many of the most fearsome Egyptian deities were female—although many goddesses had two distinct sides to their character and could also be protective and benign if sufficiently placated.

LEFT **This 30th-dynasty relief scene shows Nakhtnebef (Nectanebo) I, wearing the Red Crown of Lower Egypt, offering Ma'at (the goddess embodying truth and harmony) to the baboon form of the god Thoth.**

The task of protecting the pharaoh himself was undertaken by the twin goddesses Nekhbet and Wadjet, "the Mighty Ones." Nekhbet, the vulture goddess of Upper Egypt, shielded the king with her outstretched wings, her northern counterpart being Wadjet, the cobra goddess of Lower Egypt, who spat fire into the eyes of the king's enemies. The pharaoh wore images of both goddesses on his brow and his relationship with them was emphasized in the royal title "He of the Two Ladies."

RIGHT **One of the jeweled pectorals of Tutankhamun featuring the "Two Ladies," the twin goddesses Nekhbet, the vulture goddess of Upper Egypt (left), and Wadjet, the cobra goddess of Lower Egypt (right). They wear the respective white and red crowns of the Two Lands and use their wings to protect the king, who is shown in the form of Osiris, with whom every pharaoh was identified after death.**

The king was also guarded by the lioness goddess Sekhmet, "the Powerful One," who directed the forces of aggression and destruction. She was the daughter of the sun god, and in her vengeful aspect she was called "the Eye of Re," the one who slaughters Re's enemies with her fiery breath. Her association with the blood of battle is reflected in her title "Lady of Red Linen." Sekhmet could cause pestilence and disease, and her

The face of the goddess Hathor from her cult center of Dendera; this column capital uses the frontal aspect of the human face framed by her distinctive coiffure. The cow ears holding back her copious hair symbolize the goddess's bovine nature.

priests were trained in medicine in order to counteract her powerful effects.

Originally regarded as an aspect of Sekhmet, the goddess Bastet was eventually tamed into the form of the much-loved domestic cat. She was worshiped predominantly at Bubastis in the Delta, and recent examination of the huge numbers of cat mummies buried here and at Sakkara has revealed that many had been bred especially to be offered back to the goddess.

Another female deity associated with warfare was the ancient northern goddess Neith, "Mistress of the Bow, Ruler of Arrows," who was represented by a shield with crossed arrows. She was a goddess of astute judgment, sought by the other gods. Some late texts say that Neith spat out the evil underworld serpent Apep, the enemy of Re, although elsewhere she is imagined as the sun god's mother and protector.

The scorpion goddess Selket was another maternal protector of the king. The hippopotamus goddess Taweret ("the Great One") protected women in childbirth, and despite her ferocious appearance—designed to frighten away malevolent spirits—she was regarded as benign.

The nurturing aspect of the cow was adopted for one of Egypt's most popular goddesses, Hathor, who was portrayed either in bovine form or as a human figure with a horned crown with sun disk to represent her role as daughter of the sun god, the benign aspect of the fierce lioness Sekhmet. Such blending of goddesses can also be seen in the way in which Hathor's cult was gradually absorbed into that of Isis—for example, both were regarded as the mother of the king and often shared regalia and symbolism. Hathor herself is generally referred to as the goddess of love and beauty, and also as "the Mistress of Drunkenness" who oversaw music, dancing, and revelry in general. As "the Lady of the West," this much-loved and joyful goddess received the souls of the dead into the afterlife.

RIGHT **This gilded figure of the goddess Selket was found in the tomb of Tutankhamun. The scorpion goddess's powers were invoked to heal poisonous bites and stings, and her priests specialized in treating such ailments. Selket was also associated with the funerary cult and the embalming process, and together with Isis, Nephthys, and Neith, she protected the mummified viscera of the deceased after they had been removed from the body.**

DENDERA: HOUSE OF HATHOR

The temple of Dendera in Upper Egypt was the center of the cult of the multifaceted goddess Hathor (see page 61) from the time of the Old Kingdom. The existing temple of Dendera dates mainly from the Greco-Roman Period and is one of the best preserved in the whole of Egypt—complete with hypostyle hall, zodiac ceiling (see page 36), crypt, and sanatorium.

The rear exterior wall of the temple (right) carries a huge relief scene of the famous queen Cleopatra VII (51–30 BCE) and Caesarion, her son by the Roman leader Julius Caesar. Carved soon after Caesar's assassination in 44 BCE, the scene has recently been interpreted as expressing Cleopatra's desire to be seen as the goddess Isis, who was left to raise her child Horus alone, following the murder of her husband Osiris. By the time of Cleopatra, Isis and Hathor had merged to become a single, benign goddess of motherhood and fertility.

THE DIVINE MOTHER

Ultimately the greatest of all the goddesses, Isis came to be regarded as the most powerful figure in the Egyptian pantheon, and as the Egyptian deity par excellence. By Roman times her cult had become international, with temples of the goddess on three continents. Isis was even worshiped in the imperial outpost of Britain—courtesy of her devotees in the Roman army.

Isis was a goddess of enormous magical powers and was said to be "more powerful than a thousand soldiers," and "more clever than a million gods." In the story of Isis and Osiris (see page 68), it is Isis who takes the dominant role in resurrecting the dead Osiris by means of her magic. Isis was "the Mistress of the Gods, who knows Re by his own name"—using her guile, she was said to have tricked the sun god Re into revealing his secret name, knowledge of which brought limitless power.

Isis employed her great might to protect her young son Horus, with whom she is often depicted to emphasize her role as devoted mother. This role was frequently invoked in magical spells to protect children. Isis was also regarded as the symbolic mother of the king, "the living Horus" on earth. This royal connection is reflected in Isis' name, which means "the Throne." The hieroglyph for "throne" (𓊨) forms the goddess's crown, although she is also portrayed wearing the horned crown of Hathor, with whom Isis was closely connected and whose cult—like those of many other goddesses—she eventually absorbed.

Isis appears in her maternal protective capacity with her sister Nephthys on sarcophagi, protecting the mummy within, and the two goddesses are joined by Neith and Selket (see page 61) as the protectors of the embalmed viscera of the deceased.

Isis was worshiped throughout Egypt, with important shrines at Giza, Thebes, Abydos, and Dendera, but the center of

LEFT Isis nurses the infant Horus in this Late Period faience figurine. The form of the sculpture resembles the Egyptian hieroglyph for "throne"—the meaning of the name Isis. As her cult spread throughout the Roman world, such depictions of the goddess and her infant son became widespread and served as the model for Christian representations of the Virgin and Child.

RIGHT From the New Kingdom onward, Egypt's two greatest goddesses were often portrayed virtually identically, to the extent that they could almost be regarded as manifestations of a single goddess, Isis-Hathor. This representation of the goddess in her Hathor aspect comes from the beautifully carved and painted tomb of King Horemheb (ca. 1319–1292 BCE).

her cult was in the far south on the island of Philae in the Nile, a place once believed to be the source of the river itself. The present temple buildings of Philae are relatively late, dating from the 25th dynasty (760–656 BCE) to Roman times.

Because of its remote southerly location, Philae was able to function well into the Christian era, and indeed it was the last pagan temple in Egypt. The Roman empire ordered the closure of all non-Christian places of worship in 392 CE, but the cult of Isis at Philae was fully replaced by Christian worship in 551 CE, at which time many images of the old gods and goddesses were defaced. Philae is also the site of the last datable hieroglyphs, roughly carved on August 24, 394 CE. There are also graffiti at Philae in demotic, the popular written form of ancient Egyptian, dating from 452 CE—long after most Egyptians had converted to Christianity and were using the Greek-based Coptic script.

LEFT "Trajan's Kiosk," once known as "Pharaoh's Bed," is a ceremonial landing stage built on the east side of Isis's cult center at Philae by the Roman emperor Trajan in the 1st century CE. The top of each central gateway is cut away to allow tall ritual standards bearing sacred emblems to be carried through during processions.

LEFT Isis was one of the divine protectors of the dead. Here, she kneels with arms outstretched in a gesture of protection on the gilded coffin of Thuya, the mother-in-law of Amenhotep III (see page 10).

THE BATTLES OF HORUS

The falcon god Horus was "Lord of the Sky" and the god of the east. His eyes were the sun and moon, and as Harakhty ("Horus of the Horizon"), he was linked with the sun god in the form Re-Harakhty. Usually depicted as a falcon or as a falcon-headed man, Horus was the son of Isis and Osiris. His parents had ruled Egypt together until Osiris was murdered by his jealous brother Seth, the Lord of Chaos, who seized the throne. The grieving Isis restored her husband's dismembered body by magic, and conceived their son Horus. She raised the infant Horus (known to the Greeks as Harpocrates, or "Horus the Child") in secret. The adult Horus (Haroeris, or "Horus the Elder") set out to avenge his father and reclaim the throne as his rightful inheritance.

In the story of the battles of Horus and Seth, Horus first took his case to the gods, all of whom supported his claim—except for the sun god Re, who believed Seth, as the fiercer and stronger god, should keep the throne. Unable to come to a unanimous decision, the gods appealed to the great goddess Neith, who decided in favor of Horus. The gods duly awarded him the throne, but Seth disputed their decision and challenged his nephew to physical combat. The result was a series of ferocious battles, depicted in reliefs at the temple of Horus at Edfu.

During their titanic struggles, Seth cut out Horus's left eye, which was restored by the goddess Hathor. Once again, Horus appealed to Neith, while Osiris spoke to Re from the underworld and threatened to unleash the spirits of retribution if justice was not done. And so the gods finally restored Horus to his throne. Seth accepted the decision and thenceforward used his formidable energies to assist Re in the fight against the forces of darkness.

LEFT This small glazed amulet-like figurine represents Horus the child riding on a donkey (19th to 22nd dynasties, ca. 1295–715 BCE).

RIGHT **In the main courtyard of the temple of Edfu, Horus's cult center, stands this colossal granite figure of the falcon god wearing the double crown of a united Egypt. Like most of the temple, the statue dates from the Ptolemaic Period.** **(See also pages 104–7.)**

As Horus ruled Egypt, the land of the living, so Osiris became the ruler of the underworld, the land of the afterlife. Every pharaoh was revered as "the Living Horus," the incarnation of Horus on earth. The king continued his royal role after death when he descended to the underworld to become united with Osiris.

THE EYE OF HORUS

During the struggle for the throne of Egypt (see page 68), Seth is said to have gouged out Horus's left eye, which symbolized the moon. In other versions of this story, Seth rips out both eyes and buries them in the desert, where they grow into lotus flowers. In both versions, the goddess Hathor restores Horus's sight using a magical potion. The Eye of Horus therefore came to represent the power of healing, and its name, *wedjat*, means "sound," or "whole." Horus is depicted as a falcon and as a falcon-headed man (left)—the form of the *wedjat* resembles the eye markings of a falcon. The *wedjat* was seen as a potent amulet and was often worn as protective jewelry.

THE SONS OF RE

LEFT The gold funerary mask of Tutankhamun (ca. 1332–1322 BCE) was found in the pharaoh's tomb in the Valley of the Kings. The mask captures the young king's beautiful features and portrays him with heavily made-up eyes and pierced ears. His face is framed by the traditional striped *nemes* headcloth, crowned with the protective *uraeus* (cobra) and vulture goddesses.

RIGHT This colossal head of Ramesses II (ca. 1279–1213 BCE) marks the entrance to the temple of Luxor. Like Tutankhamun (left), the king is depicted with eye makeup, pierced ears, and headcloth. However, Ramesses' fleshier features are very different from those of his predecessor and are typical of royal portraits of the Ramesside era.

The king stood at the heart of the Egyptian world. As an absolute monarch his command was law, and it was at his behest and in his name that taxes were gathered, justice was administered, and wars were waged. However, Pharaoh was more than simply a head of state. He was essential for the maintenance of cosmic order (*ma'at*)—without him Egypt would descend into chaos. Pharaoh was the mediator between humans and the celestial realm of the gods and goddesses, whose divinity he shared and from whom he derived his power. Descended from the sun god Re, the king was identified in life with Horus and in death with Osiris, ruler of the underworld.

LORDS OF THE TWO LANDS

The king of Egypt, or pharaoh—a word derived from the Egyptian word *per-aa*, which originally meant "great house," or "palace"—was the central figure in Egyptian life, the counterpoise between the mortal and divine worlds and the upholder of order. The Egyptians believed that in the beginning they were ruled by the gods themselves. In one myth, the sun god Re was the first king, ruling over a golden age of plenty. But when he grew old, his human subjects began to question his right to rule and to plot against him, so he sent his daughter—the avenging Eye of Re—to destroy the traitors. He abandoned the world for a celestial realm, and humankind fell from grace and began to fight among themselves at the loss of the sun. Seeing the chaos below, Re sent Thoth, the god of wisdom, to restore order, before appointing a succession of gods to rule as king in his place: Shu, Geb, and then Osiris.

In the myth of the Ennead (see page 38), Osiris was the first king of Egypt, inheriting the right to the throne as the firstborn of the four offspring of Geb and Nut. Osiris and Isis, his sister and queen, presided over an era of peace and prosperity in which they brought wisdom to humankind. Osiris was murdered by his jealous brother Seth, who usurped the throne until Horus, Osiris's son, finally took back the crown (see page 68).

Horus was the last god to rule Egypt. He was succeeded by human rulers known as "the Followers of Horus," but by the time of Narmer—the legendary king who was said to have united the two lands of Upper and Lower Egypt (see page 78)—all Egyptian kings were identified with the god as "the Living Horus."

The story of Osiris and Horus underpinned the Egyptian ideal that succession should be from father to son. Thus every king showed great filial piety toward the ruler he had succeeded, whether the previous pharaoh was his real father or not:

LEFT This painted wooden statuette of Senwosret I (ca. 1919–1875 BCE) was found near his pyramid at modern el-Lisht. He carries a scepter and wears the White Crown of Upper Egypt.

RIGHT From the tomb of Horemheb (ca. 1319–1292 BCE) in the Valley of the Kings, this painted wall scene depicts the 18th-dynasty pharaoh wearing the *nemes* headcloth (center). Horemheb is flanked by the goddess Isis (wearing the regalia of Hathor) and her son Horus (wearing the dual Red and White Crown of Upper and Lower Egypt).

the new king was the chief officiant at his predecessor's funeral and regarded it as his duty to complete his monuments.

An important element of Egyptian kingship was the concept that the king was of divine birth, the result of a liaison between the queen mother and the god Amun-Re. This conferred on him the divine right to rule, which he repeatedly confirmed through the performance of temple rituals (in his capacity as the country's high priest) and the celebration of special royal religious festivals.

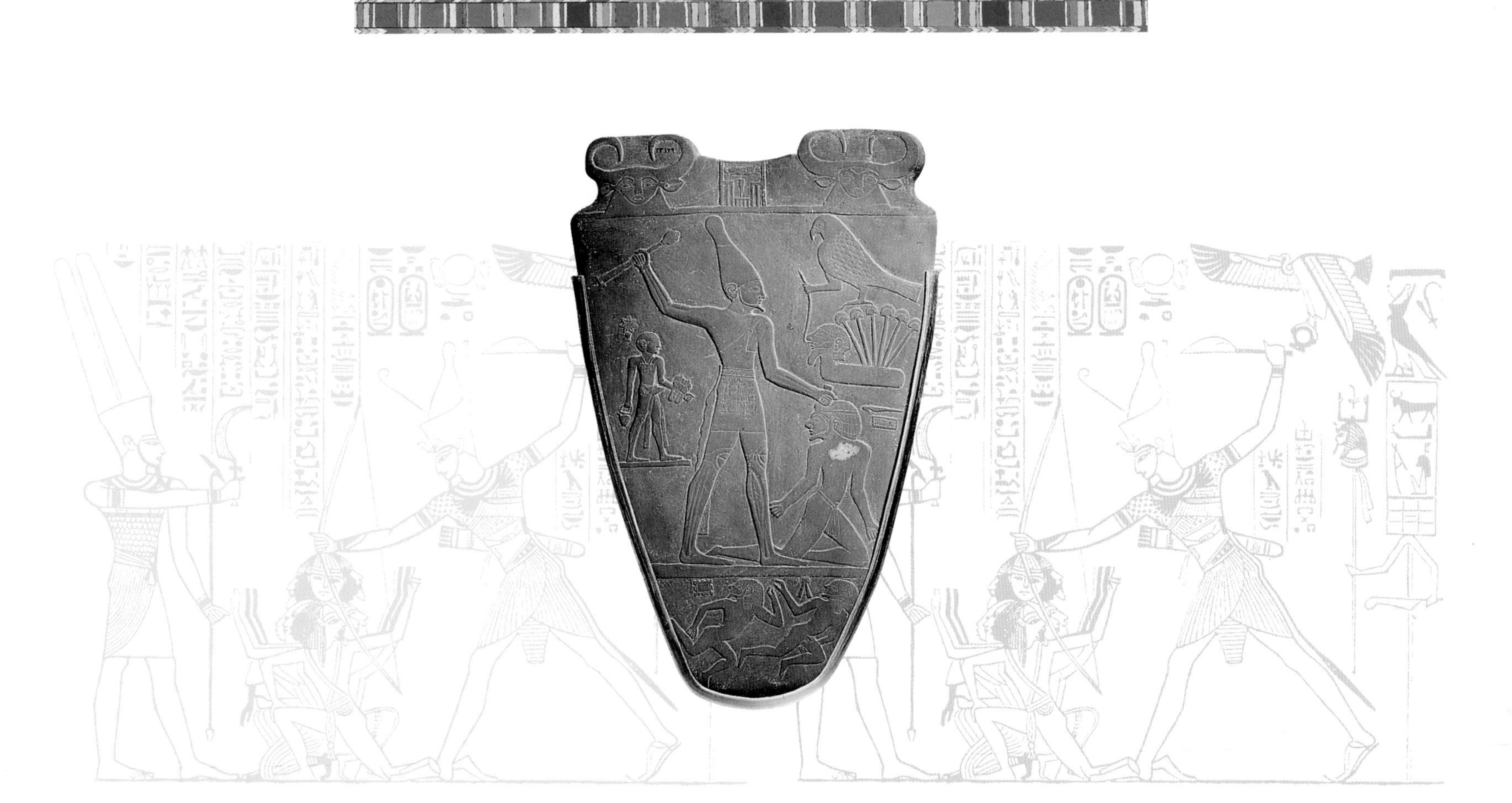

SMITING THE FOE

It was the king's duty to uphold order by overcoming Egypt's enemies and the pharaoh is always portrayed as victorious against his adversaries. The standard pose of royal invincibility is known as "Smiting the Foe," in which the pharaoh is shown poised to strike the fallen enemy, whom he holds by the hair (left). The scene—which was depicted in more or less the same form from the 1st dynasty (as on the slate palette of King Narmer, above) right through to the Roman Period—captures the most dramatic and suspenseful moment, with the king raising his mace before striking the death blow.

THE SUN KINGS

After the reigns of Egypt's predynastic rulers (the "Followers of Horus"), Upper and Lower Egypt were united for the first time ca. 3000 BCE when King Narmer of Upper Egypt defeated the chief of Lower Egypt and became the ruler of a single kingdom. The unification of the country also marks the beginning of Egypt's written history: hieroglyphic script first appeared in this period. The new writing was employed in the growing bureaucracy necessary to organize and run the state from the capital city of Memphis, which Narmer's successors established at the apex of the Delta.

Although the kings of the late predynastic and early dynastic periods were buried at Abydos, reflecting their southern origins, 3rd-dynasty rulers chose to be buried near their capital in the Memphite necropolis of Sakkara. Here, the step pyramid complex of Djoser—the first of Egypt's many pyramids—encapsulates the power of the monarchy in stone (see pages 44–49). Increasingly ambitious building schemes were undertaken. King Snofru (ca. 2625–2585 BCE), the founder of the 4th dynasty, which marked the beginning of the Old Kingdom, built three pyramids, including the first true pyramid, the so-called "Red Pyramid," at Dahshur.

Subsequent rulers of the Old Kingdom went on to construct massive pyramid complexes at Giza. The first and largest of these—the Great Pyramid—was built by Snofru's son Khufu (Cheops), about whom very little is known: his only likeness is a tiny ivory figurine (see page 8) and the extant accounts of his life are largely fictional. Close to the Great Pyramid lies that of Khufu's son Khafre (Chephren), where a stunning life-size figure was found representing Khafre held in the protective wings of the god Horus, with whom all kings identified. At this point, royal devotion to the sun god—so clearly demonstrated by the pharaohs' pyramid monuments—is also expressed in the adoption of the royal title *sa-re*, "Son of Re."

LEFT Found in the valley temple of Menkaure (ca. 2532–2510 BCE) were five triad statues depicting the king flanked by the goddess Hathor and a figure representing one of Egypt's administrative districts—here, the jackal standard represents the 17th district. The king is shown wearing the White Crown of Upper Egypt.

RIGHT The sun bursts through the clouds above the pyramids of Khufu, Khafre, and Menkaure at Giza. These massive monumental structures were intended to serve as lasting reminders of the greatness of the pharaohs who built them.

The smallest of the three Giza pyramids was built by Khafre's son Menkaure (Mycerinus). Additions made to the complex during the 5th and 6th dynasties indicate that Menkaure's cult flourished for hundreds of years after his death.

A decline in royal power occurred during the 6th dynasty. By the death of Pepy II (ca. 2288–2194 BCE), who, at the end of his extremely long reign, had come to be seen as an aging, weakened old man rather than as an omnipotent god on earth, royal power was severely undermined. Provincial officials began to create their own petty kingdoms and the country gradually fragmented until central authority broke down into the anarchy of the First Intermediate Period.

THE GUARDIAN IN THE SAND

As the earliest monumental sculpture from dynastic Egypt, the first and most famous of the country's numerous sphinxes reclines before the pyramid of Khafre (ca. 2555–2532 BCE), whose face it bears atop its leonine body. The Great Sphinx of the Giza necropolis faces the rising sun—a silent witness to more than 1,660,000 sunrises during the course of the past four and a half millennia. By the New Kingdom, however, this magnificent monument had fallen into disrepair. It was restored by Thutmose IV (ca. 1400–1390 BCE) while he was still a prince—a gesture for which he was rewarded with the throne of Egypt. According to a stela that Thutmose erected between its paws, the Sphinx appeared to the prince in a dream and promised him the throne if he cleared away the sand that had almost engulfed the monument.

IN FEAR OF HORUS

Following a century of division and civil war during the First Intermediate Period, Egypt was reunited under the southern warrior princes of Thebes (modern Luxor). Nebhepetre Mentuhotep II (ca. 2008–1957 BCE) finally defeated his northern rivals, who had made Herakleopolis their capital. Under the 11th-dynasty kings, the previously provincial town of Thebes became the most important city in the land, and the status of the local god, Amun of Karnak, was significantly enhanced. Mentuhotep embarked upon ambitious building schemes, including the construction of an imposing terraced funerary temple below the cliffs at Deir el-Bahari on the Theban west bank, behind which he and the royal women were buried.

Although subsequent pharaohs of the Middle Kingdom moved back north to the traditional capital of Memphis, they continued to add to Mentuhotep's achievements and, under the capable rule of kings, such as Senwosret III and Amenemhet III, the country thrived. Their successful military campaigns consolidated and expanded Egypt's borders, which the army defended from a series of fortresses. Successive regimes also strengthened and centralized the bureaucracy to reduce the power of regional governors (nomarchs). In terms of art and literature, this prosperous time is regarded as the "classical" period of Egyptian culture. Large-scale projects, such as land reclamation and the erection of impressive pyramids, heralded the monarch's return to absolute power. Royal portraiture depicted mighty rulers with stern, careworn faces reflecting the burdens of kingship.

The first seven kings of the 12th dynasty (four named Amenemhet and three named Senwosret) enjoyed a continuous father-son succession until Amenemhet IV died without an heir. He was succeeded by the second of Egypt's female pharaohs, his sister Sobekneferu.

LEFT This imposing black granite statue shows Senwosret III (ca. 1836–1818 BCE) wearing the *nemes* headcloth and a pleated kilt, upon which his hands (now missing) are placed in a gesture of prayer. His large ears may symbolize his vigilance.

RIGHT These jeweled pectorals, which are made of gold set with carnelian, lapis lazuli, and amethyst, belonged to a Middle Kingdom princess called Mereret. Both pectorals feature the protective vulture goddess Nekhbet. In the smaller pectoral, two griffins bear the name of the princess's father, Senwosret III, while the lower pectoral displays that of her brother, Amenemhet III (ca. 1818–1772 BCE), who is twice depicted poised to smite the foe (see page 77).

The instability caused by the long series of ephemeral monarchs under the following dynasties—around seventy kings in 150 years—led to continuous infiltration by Asiatic settlers. Absorbed into Egyptian society and ultimately also the government, Asiatics eventually took the throne ca. 1640 BCE and were known to the native Egyptians as "Hyksos" ("Rulers of Foreign Lands"). They reigned in the north while Thebes remained independent in the south, and thus Egypt entered its Second Intermediate Period. The Theban princes struggled against the Hyksos until Egypt was finally reunited under the Thebans by Ahmose (ca. 1539–1514 BCE).

THE AGE OF EMPIRE

The start of the 18th dynasty under King Ahmose (ca. 1539–1514 BCE) marks the beginning of the New Kingdom, a period known as the "Golden Age" of ancient Egypt. After the expulsion of the Hyksos, vigorous campaigning continued, as a series of unrelenting warrior-pharaohs created the greatest empire yet seen. At its center stood Thebes, its local god Amun elevated to the status of a national deity.

Ahmose was succeeded by his son Amenhotep I, who followed in his father's military footsteps to pacify Nubia. He also founded the village of Deir el-Medina for the workers who built the royal tombs in the Valley of the Kings, burial site of the New Kingdom rulers. The following three monarchs, all called Thutmose, were the sons of non-royal women, and strengthened their claims to the throne by marrying into the female royal line. On the sudden death of Thutmose II (ca. 1482–1479 BCE), his heir was still too young to rule, and so the widowed queen, Hatshepsut, reigned as pharaoh for twenty peaceful and prosperous years. She was succeeded by her stepson and nephew, Thutmose III—the so-called "Napoleon of Ancient Egypt"—who expanded the Egyptian empire into Asia as far north as the Euphrates. His son Amenhotep II, a great soldier like his father as well as an accomplished athlete, consolidated Egypt's control over the vassal states of the Levant.

Egypt had become the most powerful country in the ancient world, its victories cemented by diplomatic alliances. As foreign tribute poured in to the royal coffers, successive pharaohs donated ever larger sums as offerings to the state god Amun of Karnak. As a result, Amun's clergy began to accumulate wealth and power to rival that of the monarchy itself.

LEFT This green schist figure of King Thutmose III (ca. 1479–1425 BCE) was discovered beneath Karnak temple, a building the pharaoh embellished throughout his long reign using tribute from the Egyptian empire, which he expanded and consolidated.

RIGHT The scenes on this painted wooden casket from the tomb of Tutankhamun (ca. 1332– 1322 BCE) depict the king triumphing over the forces of chaos, here represented by Syrian adversaries. The Egyptians are portrayed in neat, well-disciplined ranks, while the enemy troops are shown in total disarray to suggest their incompetence and inferiority.

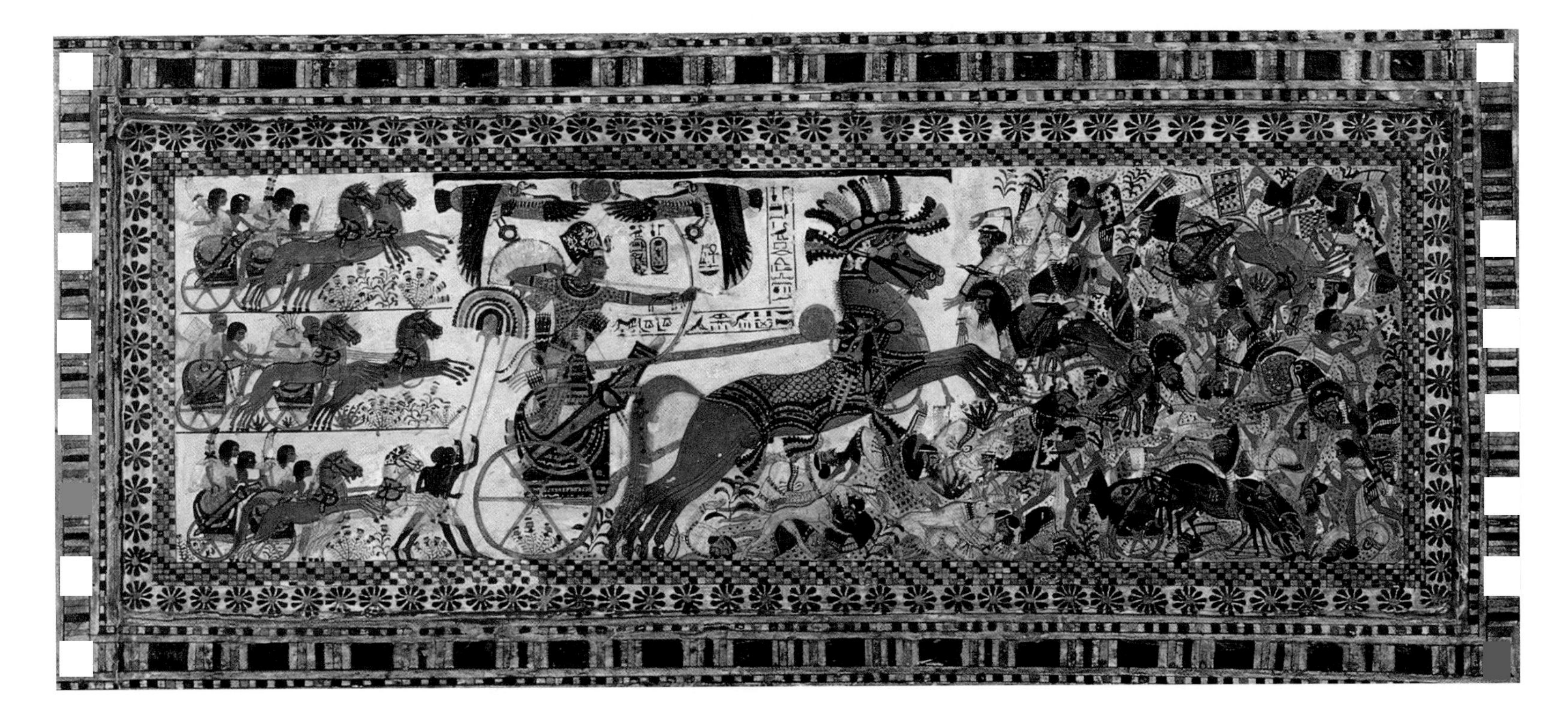

Upon the accession of one of Amenhotep II's younger sons as Thutmose IV, the power of the Karnak priests began to be curtailed. Thutmose IV's son, Amenhotep III (ca. 1390–1353 BCE), further distanced the crown from the temple of Amun, favoring instead the cult of the sun in the form of the Aten disk. This process was continued by Amenhotep IV, later Akhenaten (ca. 1353–1336 BCE), whose extreme measures in promoting the Aten threatened the fabric of Egyptian culture (see page 50). In closing down the traditional temples and relocating his capital, Akhenaten created political and economic instability that brought the country close to chaos.

In the confused aftermath of Akhenaten's reign, his son and successor Tutankhamun restored order by returning to Thebes and reestablishing the worship of the traditional gods. The last king of the 18th dynasty, Horemheb (ca. 1319–1292 BCE), set about restoring Egypt's neglected empire through reconquest—an imperialistic policy that was continued by the following dynasty, typified by Sety I and his famous son, the celebrated Ramesses II (ca. 1279–1213 BCE).

FAITH AND GLORY: LUXOR

The temple of Luxor was built by Amenhotep III (ca. 1390–1353 BCE) as a place to celebrate the annual Opet festival in which the king united with his divine *ka* (spirit) to strengthen his ability to rule. During the festival, the cult statue of the god Amun was carried to Luxor from the much larger temple of Amun at Karnak to the north (see pages 54–57) along a processional way lined with sphinxes.

Amenhotep's graceful columns and interior buildings, partly decorated by his grandson Tutankhamun, were then later extended by Ramesses II (ca. 1279–1213 BCE) in an attempt to emulate his illustrious predecessor—the front pylon and first courtyard are Ramesside additions. Alexander the Great also restored and made additions to some of the interior buildings almost a thousand years later. The entrance was flanked by two obelisks until 1819, when the right-hand one was given to the French. It now stands in the Place de la Concorde in Paris, France.

In 1989 a substantial cache of superb stone statuary, including a large figure of the king as a god, was discovered beneath the floor of the court of Amenhotep III.

White Crown

Red Crown

Red and White Crown

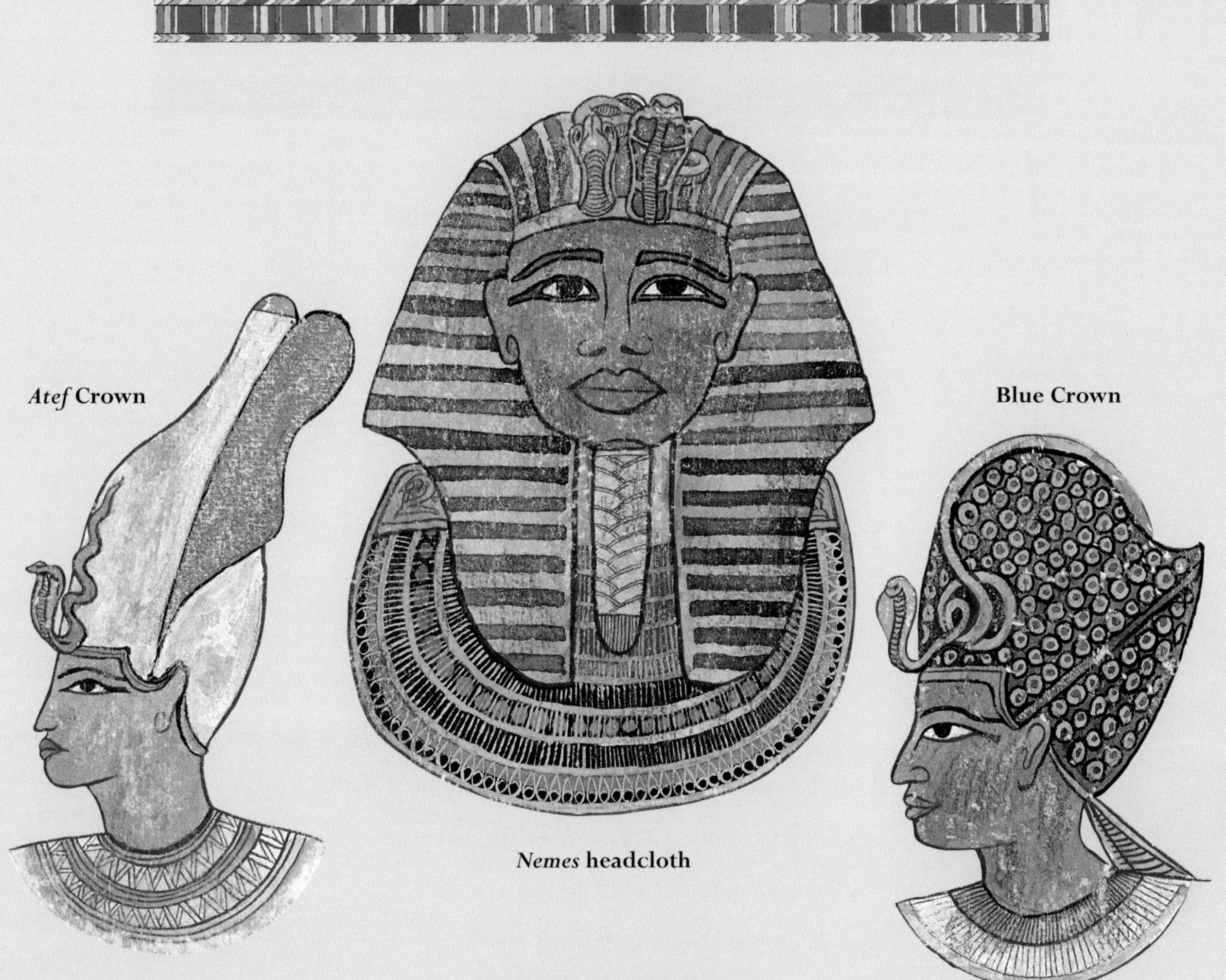

THE FACE OF POWER

Egyptian royal portraiture often displays the emblems of pharaonic power, such as the regalia of crook and flail, scepter and mace, and the many forms of regal costume. Kings were usually depicted wearing one of a large range of crowns, most of which bore the *uraeus* (sacred serpent) over the brow. Upper and Lower Egypt were symbolized by the White Crown (*Hedjet*) and Red Crown (*Deshret*) respectively, while the Red and White Crown combined (*Pschent*) represented the "Two Lands" of the united Egypt. The plumed *Atef* Crown was worn on certain ritual occasions and was associated with the god Osiris. The blue-and-yellow striped headcloth (*Nemes*)—as represented on Tutankhamun's funerary mask—was popular with rulers throughout the pharaonic period. The Blue Crown (*Khepresh*), which was linked with the sun god, was frequently worn by 18th-dynasty pharaohs.

ROYAL WOMEN

It is clear from artistic, literary, and archaeological evidence that Egyptian women were generally regarded as the equals of their male counterparts. Royal mothers and wives, such as Ramesses II's principal wife, Nefertari, enjoyed great influence and prestige. A small number of royal women even took the throne as kings in their own right: female rulers are known from a very early period. In the 2nd dynasty, there was said to be a law that permitted women to reign, although they usually acted as regents for underage sons who later became pharaohs.

Egypt's first recorded female king was the 6th-dynasty monarch Neith-ikret (ca. 2148–2144 BCE), who was long remembered as "the bravest and most beautiful woman of her time." Neith-ikret seems to have reigned on her own behalf rather than for a son, as did Sobekneferu (ca. 1763–1759 BCE), who ruled with full royal titles at the end of the 12th dynasty. As a dutiful heir, she completed the building projects begun by her father, Amenemhet III, and was represented wearing the royal *nemes* headcloth and kilt over female dress.

Three centuries later, following the early death of her husband Thutmose II ca. 1479 BCE, Hatshepsut, the daughter of Thutmose I, assumed traditional kingly regalia. After initially ruling as regent, she went on to command complete power, reestablishing long-distance trading networks, mounting several military campaigns, and constructing an impressive funerary temple.

Another famous Egyptian queen, Nefertiti, was actively involved in the reforms that replaced the traditional religious framework with the cult of the Aten. She appears twice as often as her husband, Akhenaten, in certain reliefs at Karnak and some scholars believe that Nerfertiti also ruled independently as king after Akhenaten's death ca. 1336 BCE.

LEFT This fragment of a painted limestone sculpture of Hatshepsut (ca. 1473–1458 BCE) is from her mortuary temple at Deir el-Bahari in western Thebes (see page 94). She is represented in the form of the male god Osiris, with whom all kings were identified after death.

RIGHT Nefertari, the favorite wife of Ramesses II (ca. 1279–1213 BCE), is shown making offerings to the gods in this detail of the wall paintings in her tomb in the Valley of the Queens. Ramesses also built a small temple for Nefertari at Abu Simbel.

The most famous of all the formidable Ptolemaic women who ruled Egypt was Cleopatra VII, whose twenty-one-year reign (51–30 BCE) briefly restored the country's greatness in the face of Roman aggression. Her suicide marked the end of Egypt's self-government and is often taken as the notional end of ancient Egypt.

The position of pharaoh was more commonly held by a man, so the most influential women at the Egyptian court were usually his mother, sisters, wives, daughters, and female relatives. The titles accorded to the queen—who was either the king's "Great Wife" (principal wife) or his mother—generally refer to her in relation to her husband, her son, or her children: ("Wife of the King Whom He Loves"; "Consort of Horus"; "Mother of the King"; "Mother of the King's Children"). Some queens were also known as "Mistress of the Two Lands," "Great One of the Scepter," or the somewhat less imposing "Beautiful of Appearance Upon Gazing." Like the king, the queen was regarded as semidivine and given honors befitting a goddess: queens of the Old Kingdom were buried in pyramid tombs and provided with the ceremonial boats necessary to sail the heavens with the gods. The tomb of Menkaure's daughter, Khentkawes, has been referred to as the "fourth pyramid" of Giza, because it stands before the remaining three we see today (see page 44).

LEFT During the 25th to 26th dynasties of the Late Period the high priestess based at Karnak temple played a very powerful role in Egypt—the women who bore this title controlled the south of Egypt, while their male relatives ruled from the northern capital, Memphis. This inlaid bronze figurine represents a "God's Wife of Amun," as the high priestesses were known.

The royal women associated with the 11th-dynasty king Mentuhotep II (ca. 2008–1957 BCE) were all buried close to him within his imposing funerary complex at Deir el-Bahari. The mothers, wives, and daughters of later Middle Kingdom pharaohs also had pyramid burials, and wooden caskets filled with gorgeous jewelry have been discovered in several of their tombs.

Some royal women were admired for their military prowess. The 18th-dynasty queen Ahhotep rallied Egyptian troops against the Hyksos (see page 8) after both her husband and eldest son had fallen in battle; in the words of her surviving son, Ahmose, "she cared for her soldiers, she brought back her fugitives and gathered up her deserters, she has pacified the south and expelled her rebels." In her rich burial, weapons and golden military decorations

lay beside her mirror, fan, and jewelry. The power of Queen Nefertiti is displayed in scenes in which—wearing the monarch's Blue Crown and wielding a scimitar—she is shown executing foreign prisoners.

Queen Tiy, the "Great Royal Wife" of Amenhotep III (ca. 1390–1353 BCE), achieved a level of prominence never before seen for a royal consort. While the king was worshiped as the earthly manifestation of the sun god, Tiy was regarded as Hathor, and in the goddess's guise as the fierce lioness, Sekhmet, Tiy was able to bestow everything from peace and love to divine retribution. Two of the daughters of Amenhotep and Tiy were also made "Great Royal Wives," to reflect Hathor's triple role as mother, wife, and daughter of the sun god. Such marriages helped keep power within the ruling house and reinforced the king's divine status.

LEFT This famous head of Nefertiti, wife of Akhenaten (1353–1336 BCE), shows the queen with her trademark tall Blue Crown, which she is depicted wearing when undertaking symbolic royal duties—even smiting foreign enemies—normally reserved for the sovereign himself.

Minor royal wives also wielded a certain amount of power, because they sometimes had the opportunity to influence the succession. Like the queen, they were honored with the title "Mother of the King" if their son was chosen as heir to the throne. This sometimes led to intrigue and plotting—the so-called "Harim Conspiracy," for example, resulted in the assassination attempt on the life of Ramesses III, when one of his minor wives conspired to have her son made pharaoh.

Many of the king's wives were foreign, sent to the Egyptian court in order to seal diplomatic relations. In a dispatch to one of his Asiatic vassals, Amenhotep III wrote, "Send very beautiful women—but none with shrill voices!"

THE TEMPLE OF THE GODDESS KING

Inspired by the earlier funerary temple of Mentuhotep II, which is situated at Deir el-Bahari below the Theban cliffs, the female king Hatshepsut chose to have her funerary temple built along similar lines (see page 90). Her graceful temple—designed by her architect and "Chief of Works," Senmut, who was buried nearby—was set in a series of terraces adorned with an array of delicately carved relief scenes and huge statues of the king in the guise of Osiris. The temple's central axis extends across a great forecourt, where it originally formed an avenue flanked with trees and statues of the illustrious female monarch in full pharaonic regalia. Hatshepsut's body was buried in a tomb on the other side of the cliffs in the Valley of the Kings.

WISDOM, RITES, AND MAGIC

LEFT This painted relief from the Abydos temple of Ramesses II (ca. 1279–1213 BCE) shows the androgynous Nile god Hapy making a sacred offering that represents the bounty of Egypt—fruit, vegetables, and bread.

RIGHT Dating to the Middle Kingdom, this blue-glazed faience fertility figurine represents a naked woman covered in tattoo marks and wearing a bead-and-shell hip belt. Such figures have been found in tombs and have been interpreted as aids to the regeneration of the dead.

The Egyptians believed that the performance of daily rituals was essential for the smooth-running of the universe and the maintenance of divine equilibrium. In the temples, the priesthood regularly performed rites in order to honor the gods and thank them for their continued care of the people, and a huge body of sacred wisdom developed to ensure that such rites were carried out correctly and effectively. Ordinary Egyptians venerated their favorite divinities at household shrines and invoked their protective powers in magical rituals and the amulets they wore. The mass of the people could also worship the gods directly in annual festivals, when the holy statues of deities were carried from temple to temple in grand public processions.

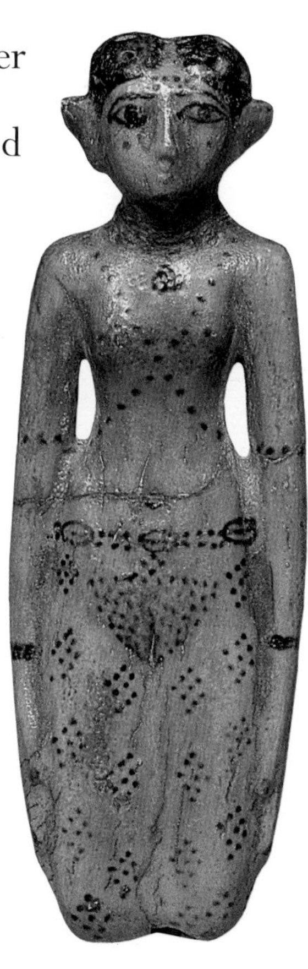

WHAT THOTH HAS WRITTEN

From the Memphite creation myth, in which the universe was created by the power of intellect alone (see page 39), it is clear that the ancient Egyptians realized the infinite possibilities and vast potential of the human mind. The Egyptian god of knowledge was Djehuty, or Thoth, who was represented as an ibis (or ibis-headed man) or as a baboon with a crown combining the crescent moon and full moon. He was generally regarded as a child of the sun god Re, who appointed him as his deputy to keep earthly affairs in order. Re allowed Thoth to give humans the knowledge of hieroglyphs, which contained all wisdom and could be used to organize and administer the country.

Since the written word was regarded as highly potent, Egypt's literate minority—educated in temple colleges called "houses of life"—were considered to have special powers. The "lector-priest" (*hery-heb*), who read out the ritual texts during temple ceremonies, was often seen as a magician, since it was he who spoke the magical "words of power." All texts used in sacred temple rituals were regarded as "books of Thoth" and were stored in temple libraries, such as those at Edfu and at Thoth's cult center, Hermopolis. By the late Roman Period, it was said that the entire knowledge of the ancient Egyptians—including mathematics, medicine, geography, astrology, and law—was contained in forty-two such books, which had been written by Thoth himself. The Greeks identified Thoth with their own god Hermes, and so began the legend of Hermes Trismegistos ("Thrice-Great Hermes/Thoth"), and his book of magic, *Hermetica*.

Repeated references to this mysterious book by ancient Greek and Latin authors intrigued scholars in Renaissance Europe, and Egypt gained a reputation as the fount of all wisdom. Since hieroglyphs could

LEFT The most trusted official of Amenhotep III (ca. 1390–1353 BCE) was Amenhotep, son of Hapu. This life-size black granite figure shows him in the pose of a seated scribe, his papyrus stretched across his lap and his paint box hanging over his left shoulder. The figure's well-rounded physique indicates a privileged lifestyle free from manual labor.

RIGHT The god Thoth is portrayed embracing Sety I (ca. 1290–1279 BCE) in this painted relief from the king's Theban tomb. Thoth is shown in human form with an ibis' head beneath a stylized wig. Sety wears the royal *nemes* headcloth.

not at that time be translated, Egypt remained a land of mystery, and the strange rites depicted on temple walls and elsewhere gave rise to much speculation.

Now that the accompanying hieroglyphic inscriptions can be read, we know that most ancient Egyptian rituals had a very specific and practical religious purpose, often far removed from the highly esoteric significance that later ages commonly ascribed to them. The "wisdom of Egypt" certainly existed, but it was a far more practical body of knowledge than has often been supposed.

RITES AND FESTIVALS

The focus of every ancient Egyptian settlement was the temple, a great center of activity that, in addition to its religious function, served as a combination of town hall, college, library, and medical clinic. However, only a priest was permitted access to the sacred inner part of the temple, which was regarded as a kind of storehouse of divine power. The role of the priest was to direct this power through rituals and to serve the gods.

The representative of the gods on earth was the king, who was thus the supreme priest of every temple. But, given that there was at least one temple in every town, he delegated his priestly duties to the high priest of each temple. Below the high priest were various ranks of clergy, from the "lector-priest"—a very senior cleric versed in the temple's secret scriptures—to those who tended the temple's sacred cattle. Many priests worked part-time for one month in every three.

LEFT **In this detail from the Book of the Dead of Anhai (ca. 1150 BCE), the priestess is depicted using a *sistrum* (sacred rattle) during a temple ritual. Her appearance is enhanced by an application of color on her eyes, lips, and cheeks and she is wearing a waist-length black wig topped with a lotus bud.**

Priests lived in their own small community attached to the temple. At Karnak, they lived beside the temple's sacred lake, an artificial pool where all priests were required to bathe twice each day and twice each night because those involved in holy rites had to be completely pure (*waab*). For the same reason, priests also had to shave all their body hair every other day and wear only pure linen robes.

Following precise procedures and rituals, the priests honored deities daily with a constant stream of food offerings, wine, perfumes, incense, and flowers. The gods would also be entertained by temple musicians and dancers: one text records rites associated with "the Golden Goddess, Hathor," in which

ABOVE Dancers, acrobats, and singers are depicted performing as part of a ritual at Karnak temple in this detail of a brown quartzite relief dated to the reign of Hatshepsut (ca. 1479–1458 BCE). Music and movement were intended to entertain the gods and drive away evil influences.

singers chanted invocations and dancers moved to the rhythmic accompaniment of the *sistrum*, a sacred rattle. Such devotions were believed to encourage the spirit of the deity to reside within the sacred statue that was kept in a shrine in the dark innermost sanctuary of the temple, to which the king and the high priest alone had access. Only by maintaining the divine presence within each temple could the cosmic order be upheld over the disorder and chaos depicted on the temple exterior.

Each morning, the purified high priest entered the dark shrine, dimly lit by flickering oil lamps. He carefully opened the sealed wooden doors of the shrine and approached the divine statue, greeting it and making offerings of perfume. With the little finger of his right hand, he anointed the deity's brow with sacred oils of cedar and myrrh. The statue would then be adorned with cosmetics and ceremonial clothing before being presented with food, drink, and huge floral bouquets—their fragrance was believed to be that of the gods themselves. Incense, used to welcome and sustain the gods and to repel malevolent spirits, was of great importance. It was made in bulk by priests in temple "perfume laboratories," where lists of aromatic ingredients were recorded on the walls.

In addition to such intimate temple rituals, to which only a few had access, more than fifty public festivals were celebrated regularly throughout the year. The Egyptians were the first to observe a 365-day calendar, which consisted of 360 days plus five great holy days to mark the birthdays of Osiris, Isis, Horus, Seth, and Nephthys. Other important feast days included the Festival of Hathor, at which the goddess's statue was taken from her shrine at Dendera and presented to the people amid joyful music and dancing in celebration of a good harvest. Similar events accompanied the wedding-like Feast of the Beautiful Meeting, when Hathor's statue traveled south from Dendera to spend two weeks with her "husband" Horus at Edfu.

Accompanied by a great retinue of priests, priestesses, musicians, and dancers,

LEFT This painted 4th-dynasty funerary relief from Giza shows Princess Nefertiabet wearing a priestly panther-skin robe and a long black wig. She is seated before an offering table laden with bread and meat; a list of offerings and the quantities involved is shown on the right.

RIGHT A detail of the Opet festival procession from the Ramesside reliefs at Luxor temple. A specially fattened bull with decorated horns is depicted being led by shaven-headed priests carrying loaves of bread.

the entire local population would turn out during these public holidays to take part in the revelry and enjoy great quantities of food and drink—drunkenness was actively encouraged as a means of honoring the gods.

The annual feast of Opet at Thebes was one of an important number of festivals designed to enhance and replenish the king's strength. During the festival, the sacred image of Amun, Egypt's national god, was borne upriver amid scenes of jubilation from the attendant crowds from Karnak to Luxor temple, where the king took part in a secret rite in the inner shrine. This was followed by his public appearance, reinvigorated and god-like, before his ecstatic subjects.

EDFU: PALACE OF THE HAWK GOD

The temple of Horus at Edfu is the best-preserved of all ancient Egyptian temples. The present buildings stand on the site of the original New Kingdom structure, which was constructed along the standard east-west axis. However, most of the surviving edifices are relatively late—they were begun by Ptolemy III in 237 BCE. The inner parts of the temple were finished by 212 BCE by Ptolemy IV, and Ptolemy VIII had completed their decoration by 142 BCE. Ptolemy IX made further additions and the external decoration was completed by Ptolemy XII in 57 BCE.

The Edfu temple has a *mammisi*—a structure associated with rituals surrounding the birth of the god Horus—carved with scenes featuring the figures of the pharaoh, Ptolemy VIII (170–164 BCE, 145–116 BCE), and his mother, wife, and child, accompanied by the god Bes, who was associated with childbirth. There are also scenes relating to the divine union between

The entrance to Edfu temple is marked by this great pylon, which is carved with huge figures representing Horus among the gods. The vertical grooves in which the temple's enormous flagpoles were once inserted are still clearly visible. Above the gateway is a solar disk flanked by a pair of *uraei* (sacred serpents).

the god Horus and the goddess Hathor, an occasion celebrated at Edfu during the annual festival called "the Feast of the Beautiful Meeting."

The temple is fronted by a massive pylon, decorated with huge figures of the king smiting his enemies, and flanked by large statues of Horus. Beyond the pylon, in the first court, various scenes depict rituals in which the monarch is purified and crowned, as well as festival processions and scenes of dancing and celebration associated with the meeting of Horus and Hathor.

In the ambulatory around the walls of the court, sunken relief scenes portray the "Triumph of Horus." In this ritual play, which was performed each year, Horus—personified by the king—defeated the forces of evil embodied in the figure of the god Seth (portrayed as a hippopotamus, which is depicted on a miniature scale in order to reduce the magical potency of the image).

On the far side of the court from the pylon is the entrance to the temple proper, flanked by two further statues of Horus. Inside, the first hypostyle (columned) hall is embellished with scenes showing the foundation ceremony of the temple complex. The hall also has its own library, which once contained texts used in sacred rituals, and a robing room, in which the priests' vestments were kept.

LEFT Beyond Edfu's entrance pylon lies the temple's first court, bordered by a columned ambulatory, the walls of which are decorated with relief scenes depicting rituals and festival performances.

RIGHT Deep within the temple is the inner sanctuary. It still contains its original shrine of polished syenite stone, in which the cult statue—a golden figure of Horus—would have once been housed, hidden behind finely carved cedarwood doors.

The second, and smaller, hypostyle hall beyond also houses storerooms for both solid and liquid offerings, as well as a wonderfully preserved perfume laboratory, the walls of which are inscribed with lengthy recipes for the preparation of the perfumes and incense that were made here for use during the daily rituals.

The temple's inner sanctuary contains the shrines in which the sacred cult statue of Horus originally resided. The statue was joined annually by the statue of Hathor, brought from the temple at Dendera for "the Feast of the Beautiful Meeting."

THE HEAVENLY REALM

The Egyptians studied the movements of the moon and stars from observatories situated on their temple roofs, and a section of the priesthood was trained in astronomy to ensure that the necessary rituals were performed at the correct hour. Stellar motifs were often used to embellish the ceilings of both temples and tombs. Many of these decorations depict the sky goddess Nut as a star-covered woman stretching out above the surface of the earth—she is often shown performing a similar act of protection over the deceased on the inside of their coffins lids (see pages 110–111).

LEFT This detail of a funerary relief scene shows the sun god Re, in his ram-headed form, journeying through the hours of the night in his "Barque of the Millions."

The dead themselves were also thought to rise up to join the ranks of the "Imperishable Stars," a term used of the stars around the Pole Star, which were visible in the night sky at all times of the year. This belief is first referred to in the Old Kingdom "Pyramid Texts." By the Middle Kingdom, sarcophagus lids were decorated with calendars illustrated with images of stars, especially Sothis (Sirius, the Dog Star), whose ascension on July 19 coincided with the beginning of the Nile inundation and marked the Egyptian New Year.

By the Middle Kingdom, the Egyptians had also identified five of the planets, and pictured them, like the Sun, in the guise of various gods sailing in their barques across the heavens: Mars was "Horus of the Horizon," or "Horus the Red"; Jupiter was "Horus who Limits the Two Lands" (or "the Glittering Star"); and Saturn was "Horus, Bull of the Sky." Mercury was identified with Seth, and Venus was "the God of the Morning." The Egyptians recognized many of the constellations that we know today, although they perceived them to represent different images. Orion—one of

RIGHT Both solar and stellar motifs are prominent in tomb and temple decoration. In the tomb of Hatshepsut's chief official, Senmut (ca. 1460 BCE), the detailed, though unfinished, tomb ceiling is painted in black and red and depicts the Egyptian heavens. Astronomical ceilings have also been found in the temples of Osiris at Abydos and Hathor at Dendera, as well as in the tombs of Sety I and Ramesses IV, VI, VII, and IX.

the most important constellations in Egyptian astronomy—was seen as a man holding a staff and was identified with the god Osiris. There is a theory that the three Giza pyramids were built to align with Orion's Belt.

The Egyptian calendar was divided into "lucky" and "unlucky" days, in accordance with the annual cycle of religious festivals and mythical events. However, astrology did not reach Egypt until the Ptolemaic Period, inspired by a combination of Babylonian and Greek beliefs. The famous Dendera Zodiac (see page 36) and a number of Roman coffins portray Nut surrounded by the newly introduced signs of the zodiac. Magical papyri from this late period also feature auspicious star signs, and there are a variety of late astrological works attributed to Thoth in his Greco-Roman guise of Hermes Trismegistos.

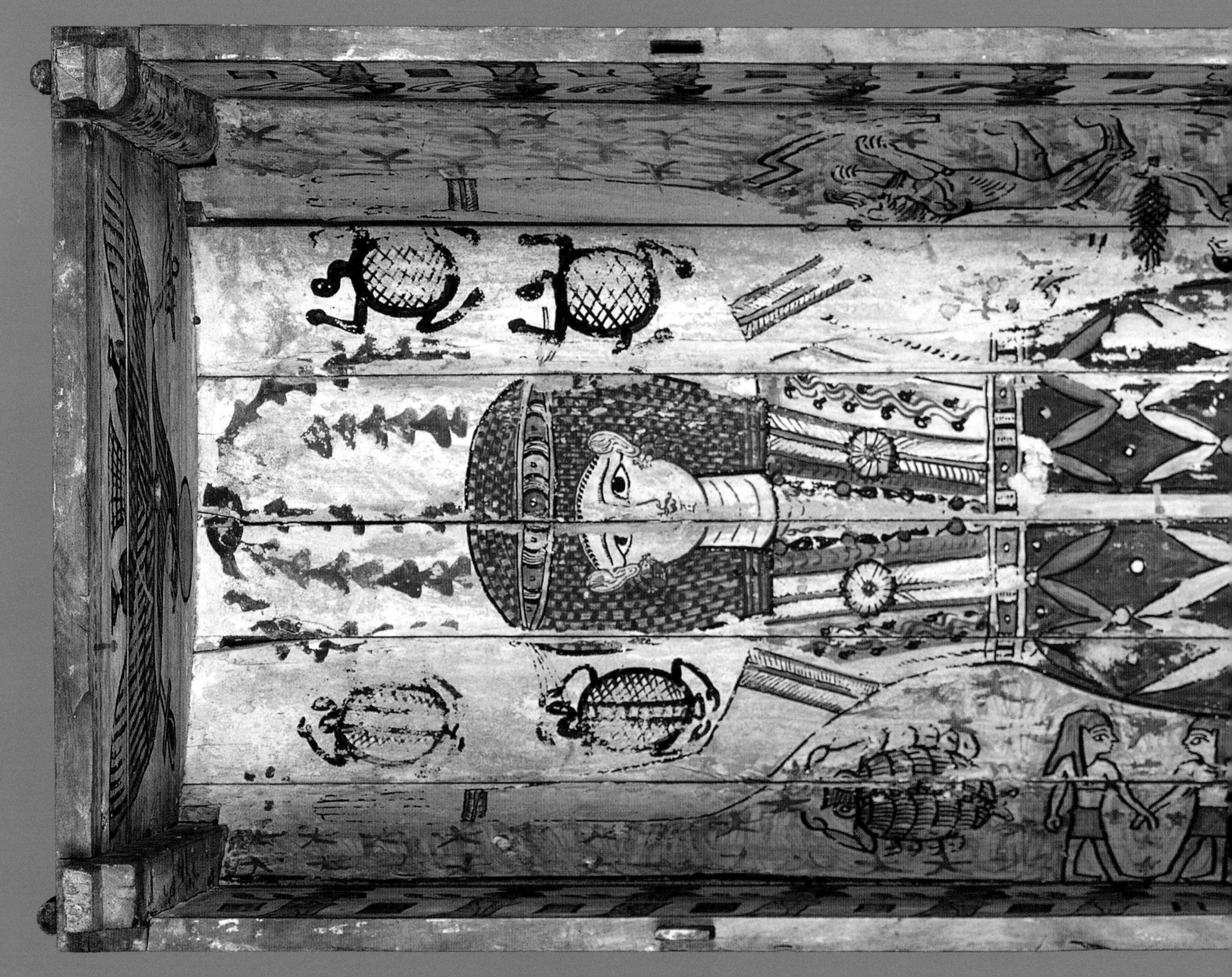

THE LADY OF THE SKIES
The interior of the painted wooden coffin lid of a young woman named Cleopatra. Aged only seventeen when she died in the early 2nd century CE, she was buried in a tomb at Qurna on the west bank at Thebes, which was shared with three generations of her family. Her painted coffin shows the Egyptian sky goddess Nut stretching out in her traditional pose over the deceased, with the sun as a red oval emitting its life-giving rays over Nut's head. References to the sky goddess

have been found in very early inscriptions, the Old Kingdom Pyramid Texts (see page 47) containing a spell that reads "O Mother Nut, spread yourself over me, so that I may be placed among the Imperishable Stars and never die." However, since this coffin dates to the latest period of ancient Egyptian history, the images are represented in a Greco-Roman style and Nut's position in the heavens among the stars is bordered by the newly introduced Babylonian-Greek zodiac, which uses the twelve horoscope symbols still familiar to us today.

MAGIC AND MYSTERIES

It is often difficult for modern observers of ancient Egypt to disentangle religion from magic. This is not surprising because for the Egyptians themselves, the distinction hardly existed. They believed it was possible to alter the world around them by directing the unseen forces of gods and spirits, and the magician's role often differed very little from that of the priest or physician. State-organized temple religion employed magical rites on a daily basis. Texts containing spells had names such as "The Book to Appease Sekhmet," "Formulae for Repelling the Evil Eye," and "The Book of the Capture of the Enemy." While these mysterious texts were being recited, the magician would often destroy wax or clay images of a person or other being perceived to threaten the divine order—such as enemies of the state or the adversaries of the sun god. The combination of the spoken word and the performance of a ritual act was believed to ensure the security of the kingdom and to restore balance to the universe.

LEFT Ornamental spoons such as this one were used for dispensing incense and perfume during temple or funerary rituals. The bowls in this example are decorated with river plants and waterfowl. Figures representing the protective household god Bes adorn the handles.

Such rites could also be practiced on a small scale for an individual's benefit, and magic was often used in a domestic context by the many ordinary Egyptians who did not have access to the temple interior. People honored both the gods and the spirits of the ancestors at household shrines, and specific spells were employed at particular times of life. It was thought especially important that childbirth be accompanied by the correct magical procedures. A pregnant woman could appeal to deities of magic, such as Bes, Taweret, and Hathor, to protect her and her child from evil spirits and ease her

ABOVE **A variety of fertility charms in the form of the hippopotamus goddess Taweret, who was known as "the Great One." Her ferocious appearance was designed to frighten away evil spirits, while her benign nature was believed to protect women in childbirth.**

labor—one spell for hastening birth implored Hathor to "send the sweet north wind." The popular dwarf god, Bes, is often shown dancing and playing instruments in his role as the protector of women in childbirth—music and noisy revelry were believed to drive away malevolent spirits.

The role of the divine mother, Isis, in protecting her son, Horus, was alluded to in spells designed to protect Egyptian children from snake and scorpion bites, burns, and other afflictions. Practical medical treatments were often prescribed alongside incantations and amulets that were believed to guard against illness.

Divination was another aspect of Egyptian magic. One ritual to invoke the god Anubis, for example, involved covering a bowl of water with a film of oil, in which images would appear to the medium. Egyptians also believed that the dead could be contacted through letters placed at their tombs requesting the help of the deceased and asking them to act as intermediaries between their living relatives and the gods.

CHARMS AND AMULETS

Magical charms and amulets were worn by both the living and the dead to repel harmful forces and bestow beneficial effects. They were produced in various materials and colors and generally took the form of popular gods, ritual objects, animals, plants, body parts, or the names of kings. The amulet shown above, ca. 1295 BCE, takes the form of a temple pylon and features the goddesses Isis (left) and Nephthys and numerous auspicious emblems: the Eye of Horus; the spine or pillar of Osiris (*djed*, 𓊽); the scarab; and the knot of Isis (*tyet*, 𓎬). The amulet necklace (opposite) includes the *djed*; *ankh* (𓋹, "life"); cowrie shell; fish (*nekhaw*, worn by children to prevent drowning); *sa* (𓍯, "protection"); and the sign for "joy" (𓈙).

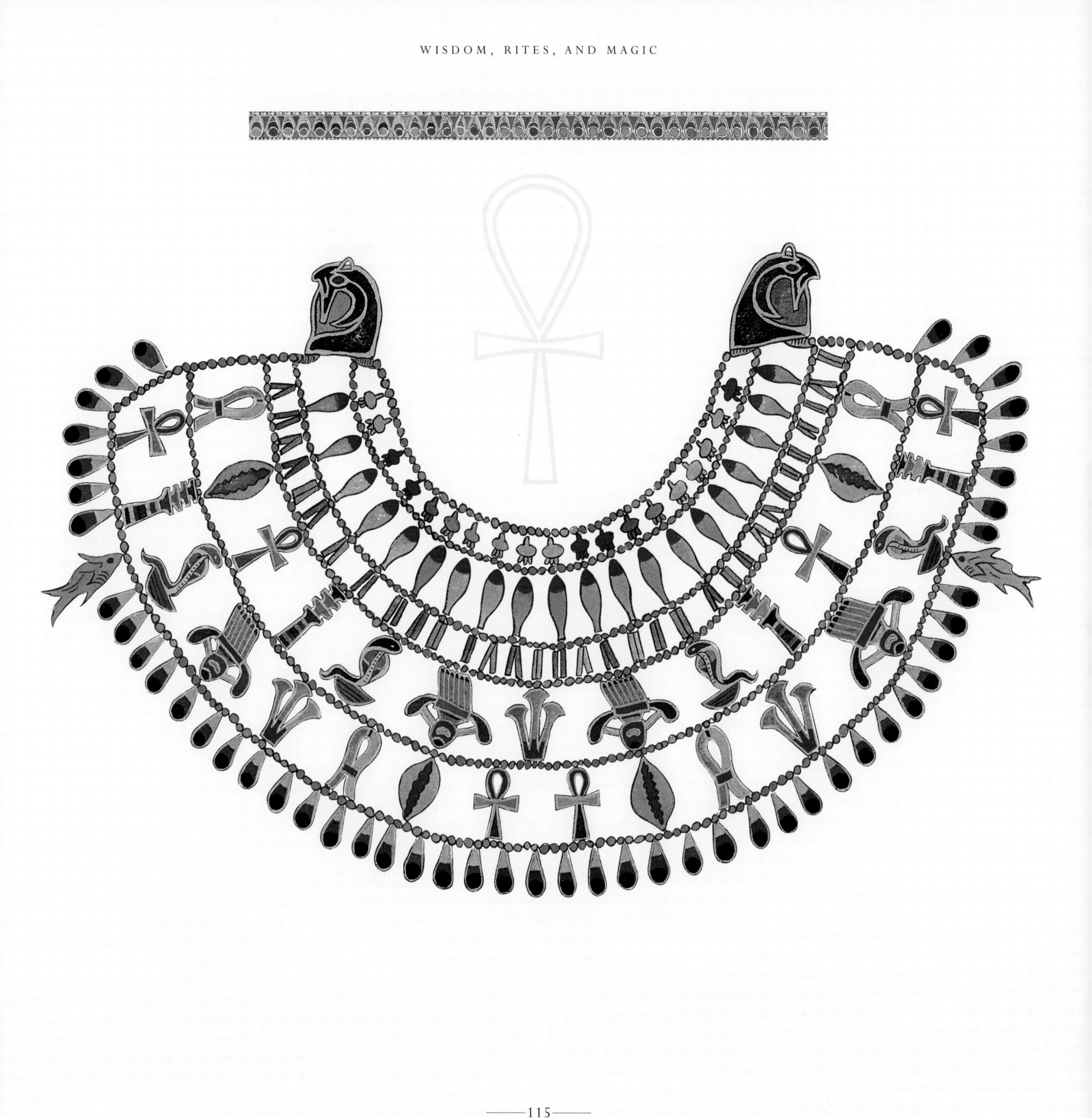

THE REALM OF OSIRIS

LEFT This detail is from the exquisitely carved basalt sarcophagus lid of Sisobek, the vizier (chief minister) of northern Egypt under Psamtik I (ca. 664–610 BCE). Sisobek wears a long tripartite wig, a plaited false beard, and a broad collar. He holds the amuletic *djed* and *sa* symbols, representing stability and protection.

RIGHT The beautifully painted 19th-dynasty tomb of Sennedjem (a tomb builder in the Valley of the Kings) lies above his home village of Deir el-Medina and contains this perfectly executed figure of Osiris. The god is shown within his shrine, holding the crook and flail of royalty and protected by a pair of *wedjat* eyes (see page 70).

The most familiar images of ancient Egypt—from mummies to pyramids—are all associated with death and burial, and the Egyptians have consequently long been thought of as a morbid people, obsessed with mortality. Yet nothing could be further from the truth. Egyptians loved life so passionately that they wanted it to last forever and did everything in their power to prolong it indefinitely. They preserved and wrapped the body, placed it in a secure tomb, and surrounded it with all the items essential for its eternal well-being in the blissful and prosperous realm of Osiris, lord of the underworld paradise.

THE SAGA OF ISIS AND OSIRIS

The story of Isis and Osiris, in which the god Osiris is resurrected from the dead, helps to explain the Egyptians' understanding of death as simply a continuation of life. At the beginning of the saga, Osiris and Isis, his sister and wife, ruled over Egypt during a golden age of peace and prosperity. But their jealous brother, Seth—the lord of chaos—envied their happiness and success, and plotted to murder Osiris and seize the throne for himself.

Seth invited Osiris to a banquet, at which he tricked his unsuspecting brother into trying out a fine coffin that he had ordered to be made. As soon as Osiris was inside, Seth sealed the coffin and flung it into the Nile—Osiris drowned and death was created.

Following the murder, the distraught Isis managed to retrieve her husband's body, only to have it snatched away from her by Seth, who savagely dismembered it and scattered the pieces far and wide across Egypt. Undeterred, Isis adopted the form of a kite and took to the skies with her sister, Nephthys, and together they managed to locate each part. The god's head, for example, was found at Abydos and his heart at Athribis. Every site at which one of Osiris's body parts was found later became a place of pilgrimage associated with his worship. Isis then reassembled Osiris' body with the help of Anubis, the god of embalming, and so produced the first mummy. All consequent mummies were believed to be protected by the god who had preceded them.

LEFT A Late Period bronze *aegis* (amulet of Isis), made up of the goddess's head topped with the horns and solar disk of Hathor and set over a broad collar carved with separate rows of beads and petals flanked by falcon-headed terminals. The piece probably served as a votive offering or was attached to a larger piece of ritual statuary.

RIGHT This scene of the resurrection of Osiris shows the god lying on a lion-headed bed (bier) while Isis standing in front of him and Nephthys standing behind him both recite spells to bring him back to life. This powerful scene is depicted on the brightly colored chest area of an Egyptian mummy mask dating from the Roman period, around the first half of the 1st century CE.

Using her immense magical powers, Isis then restored Osiris back to life and reinvigorated him temporarily so that she could conceive their son, Horus. Isis quite literally created new life from death—a miraculous act captured in a number of relief scenes and sculpture. She raised Horus in secret, and he grew up to reclaim the throne from his usurping uncle, Seth (see pages 68–69).

While Horus became the king on earth, his resurrected father, Osiris, became lord of the underworld. The embodiment of justice and righteousness, Osiris guaranteed salvation to all those who died and were judged worthy of everlasting life in the underworld paradise. For the Egyptians, he gave eternal hope to the living.

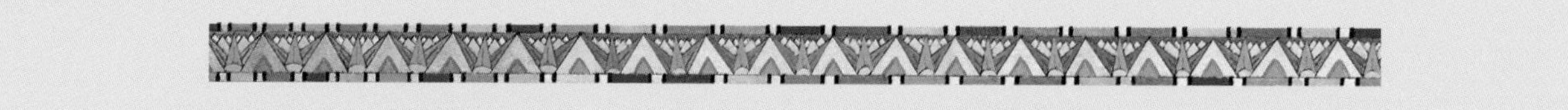

Qebsenuef Duamutef Hapi Imsety Horus

GUARDIANS OF THE DEAD

The body parts of the deceased were protected by four gods known as the Sons of Horus (standing behind their divine father, above)—guardians of the internal organs who were also linked with the four cardinal points: Qebsenuef (hawk head, guardian of the intestines, associated with the west); Duamutef (jackal head, stomach, east); Hapi (ape head, lungs, north); and Imsety (human head, liver,

Osiris **Isis** **Nephthys** **Neith** **Selket**

south). Each god was associated with, and protected by, one of the four powerful goddesses shown standing behind the throne of Osiris (above): Isis (protected Imsety and the foot end of the deceased's coffin), Nephthys (Hapi, head of coffin), Neith (Duamutef, east side of coffin), and Selket (Qebsenuef, west side of coffin). Each goddess wears her distinctive symbol as a crown.

PREPARING FOR THE AFTERLIFE

In Egyptian belief, the preservation of the corpse—mummification—was fundamental to the continuation of life after death. In the earliest period of the country's history, bodies were simply placed into hollows in the sand, where they were dessicated and preserved naturally by the hot, dry conditions. As burial practices among the elite became increasingly sophisticated, purpose-built, rectangular tombs (*mastabas*) replaced burial in the sand (see pages 44–47), and natural preservation gave way to artificial preservation techniques. The word "mummy" itself comes from *moumia*, the Persian word for "bitumen"—the substance that the Egyptians were once, wrongly, believed to have used in the preservation of bodies.

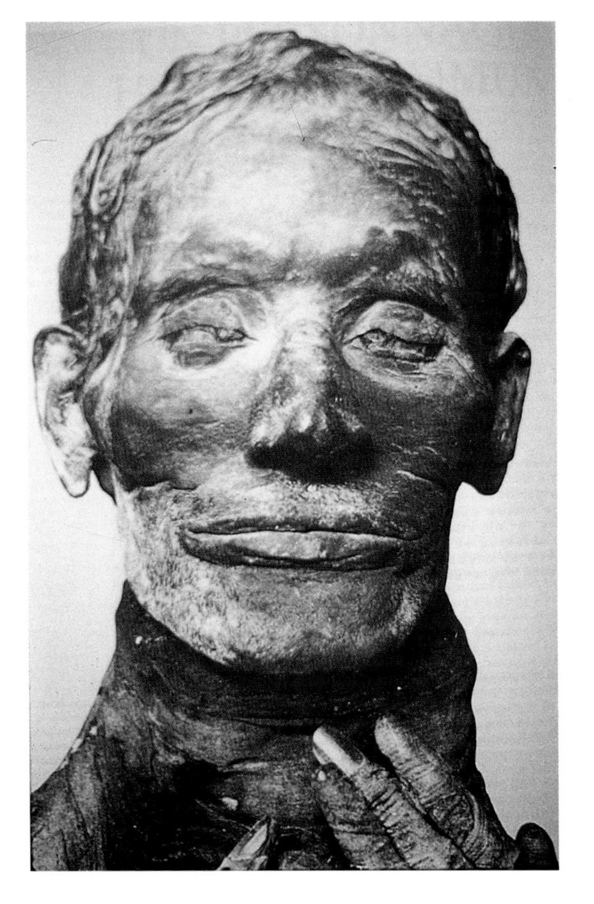

LEFT **The most perfectly preserved Egyptian mummy is that of Yuya, the father-in-law of Amenhotep III (ca. 1390–1353 BCE) and great-grandfather of Tutankhamun (ca. 1332–1322 BCE). Yuya's mummy retains its eyelashes, eyebrows, stubbly chin, carefully manicured fingernails, and blond hair.**

RIGHT **A detail of the face on Yuya's gilded coffin, in which his mummy—its head covered with a further gilded death mask—was placed. Yuya's golden face has inlaid eyes outlined in blue to represent cosmetic lines. A jeweled collar is visible on the chest.**

As the mummification process became more refined and elaborate, all internal organs, except for the heart and kidneys, were removed and preserved separately inside what are known as "canopic jars." Meanwhile, the eviscerated body was dried out beneath a layer of natron salts. The corpse was then washed and purified, the incision sewn up, and the skin anointed with a variety of oils, spices, and resins. Finally, the body was wrapped in fine linen bandages. Instructions in the "Book of the Dead"—the Egyptian "handbook" for ensuring the deceased's proper burial and safe passage into paradise—state that the dead had to be "pure, clean, clothed in fresh linen, and anointed with the finest myrrh oil," in order to enter the afterlife.

As the embalmers wrapped the body, protective amulets were placed among the bandages while priests recited the

incantations needed to activate them. Following the standard seventy-day embalming process, the prepared corpse—complete with its funerary mask depicting the deceased as living and youthful—was placed in its coffin. It was then ready for the ritual funeral procession, accompanied by priests, *muu* dancers, mourners, and servants carrying all the necessary funerary equipment.

Before the tomb, and amid clouds of purifying incense, the priests performed the "Opening of the Mouth" ceremony, essential for reanimating the *ka* (soul) and senses of the deceased. The noise and movement of music and dancing were believed to reactivate hearing and sight; incense and flowers brought back the sense of smell; and offerings of choice cuts of meat and wine enabled the deceased to

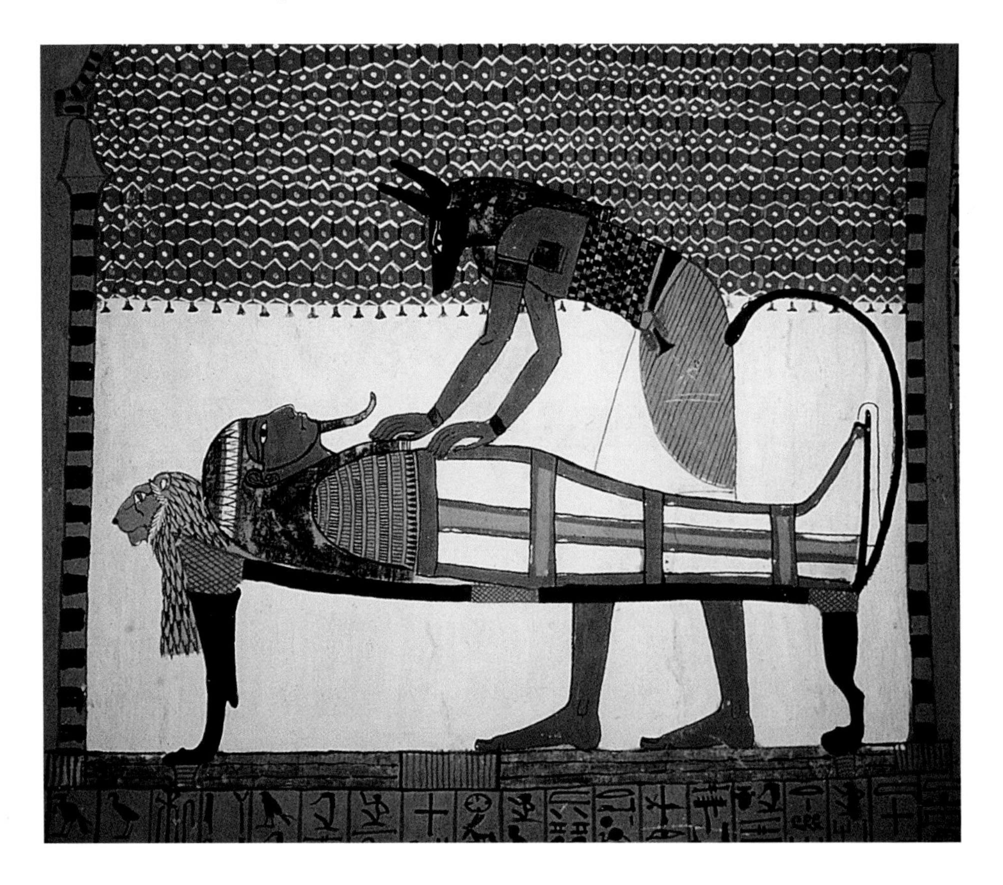

LEFT From the 19th-dynasty tomb of Sennedjem (see page 117), this detail shows Anubis, the jackal-headed god of embalming (or a priest with an Anubis mask), attending to Sennedjem's masked and wrapped mummy as it lies on a lion-headed funerary couch.

eat and drink in the afterlife. The standard offering formulae recited during this ceremony request for the deceased "a thousand of every good and pure thing for your *ka* and all kinds of offerings on which the gods live."

The reanimated mummy was then laid to rest in its tomb and surrounded by funerary objects ranging from items used in daily life to those designed specifically for burial, such as the Book of the Dead and other instructive funerary texts, and *shabtis* (magical figurines that were believed to come to life and act as servants for their owner). With the funeral complete, the deceased set out from the tomb on a hazardous journey through the underworld—which culminated in his or her judgment before the throne of Osiris, the lord of the dead (see pages 126–127).

RIGHT This scene adorns the carved limestone sarcophagus of Queen Kawit, one of the wives of Nebhepetre Mentuhotep II (ca. 2008–1957 BCE). As a hairdresser plaits Kawit's hair, which she admires in a handheld mirror, a servant offers his mistress milk, fresh from a cow depicted on a scene farther down the sarcophagus.

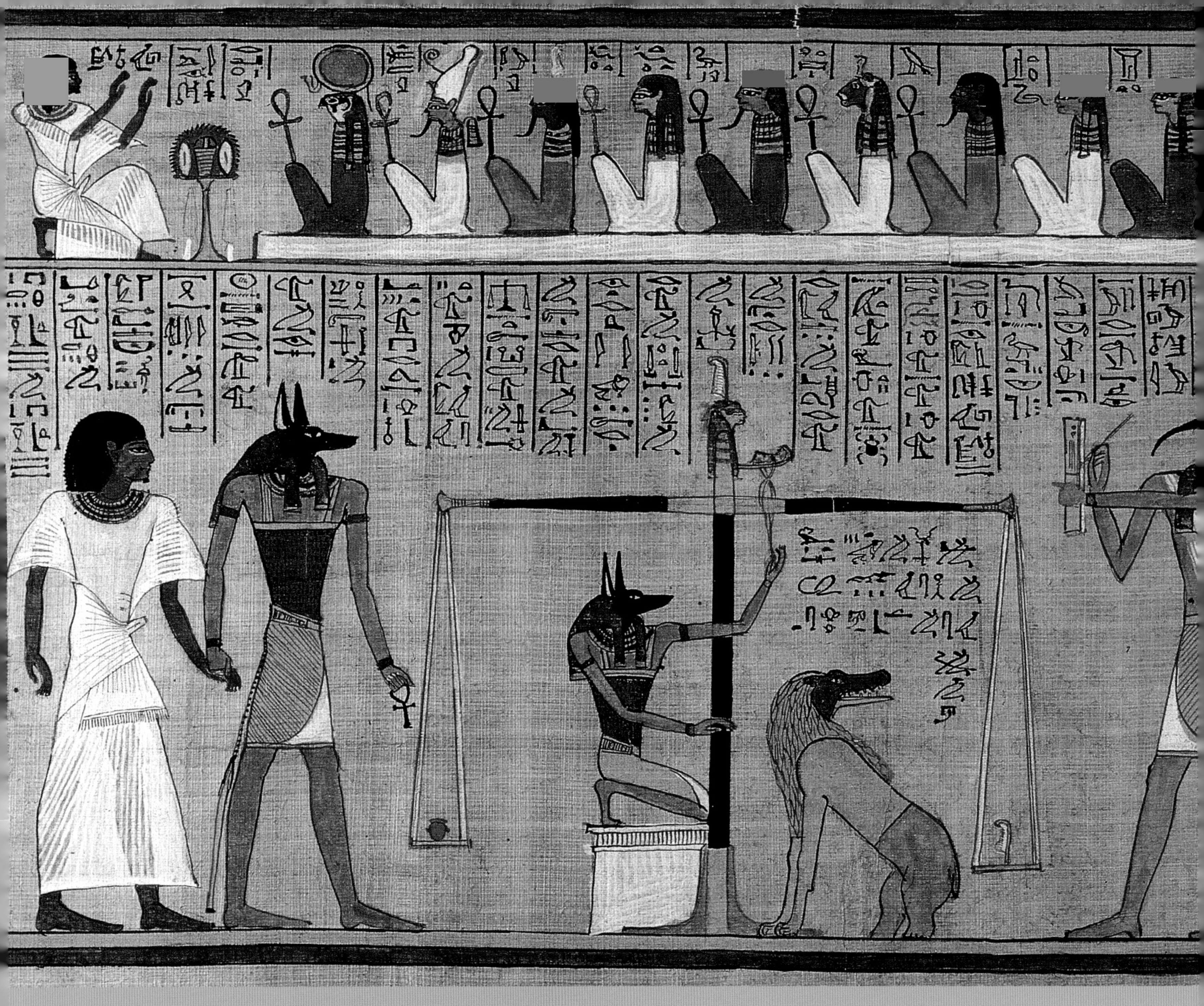

IN THE HALL OF OSIRIS

This scene is from the Book of the Dead produced ca. 1285 BCE for a royal scribe, Hunefer. It depicts the key stage in the transformation of the deceased into an *akh*—a spirit that could help its living relatives. In a chamber of the underworld called "the Hall of Two Truths," the deceased was led by Anubis before Osiris, god of the underworld and ultimate judge of the dead, and forty-two assessor gods. The deceased was presented with a long list of sins and had to deny each in turn.

Anubis tested the veracity of their denials by weighing their heart—the seat of thought and consciousness—against a feather representing Ma'at (truth). If heart and feather were of equal weight, the deceased was declared "true of voice" and "justified." Thoth recorded the judgment and Horus led the deceased to the throne of Osiris—whence they passed into the blessed afterlife. But if the heart was heavy with sin and tipped the scales, it was thrown to Ammut, a hybrid monster that annihilated evildoers by devouring their hearts.

VISIONS OF PARADISE

The Egyptians' ultimate aim was to live forever in their beloved homeland; they envisaged eternal paradise as simply a continuation of their lives on earth, albeit with a few refinements. In the idealized afterlife, the *shabti* figures (see page 125) would perform all manual work—detailed models placed in tombs often represented the kind of activities they would perform. Harvests would be enormous, and drought and illness nonexistent. The deceased and their families would enjoy banquets and boating trips, or relax in their flower gardens. An inscription on Tutankhamun's drinking cup expresses the ultimate Egyptian wish: "May your soul live, may you spend millions of years, O lover of Thebes, with your face to the north wind and your eyes beholding happiness."

To help the deceased reach blessed eternity, funerary texts acted as a kind of guidebook to the afterlife. The earliest surviving maps from Egypt are those depicting the route to the afterlife in texts known as "The Book of Two Ways," which were painted on the inside of Middle Kingdom coffins. Later incantations in the New Kingdom Book of the Dead are entitled "Spell for Not Dying a Second Time," "Spell Not to Rot and Not to Do Work in the Land of the Dead," and "Spell for Not Having Your Magic Taken Away"—as well as "Spells of Transformation," which would change the deceased's form to facilitate their passage through the underworld. One magic formula for transforming the deceased into a lotus flower states: "I am this

BELOW One of several painted wooden models discovered in the Theban tomb of the royal official Meketre (ca. 2000 BCE). The model shows the biennial counting of the cattle for tax purposes: Meketre himself is seated under a shady portico beside his scribes, who are recording the numbers of cattle being driven past.

RIGHT In this illustration, from the Book of the Dead buried with the scribe Ani (ca. 1290 BCE), the deceased is shown plowing, reaping, and threshing; sailing across the Lake of Offerings; and worshiping a range of gods including Re, the seven Hathor cows, and the Heron of Plenty.

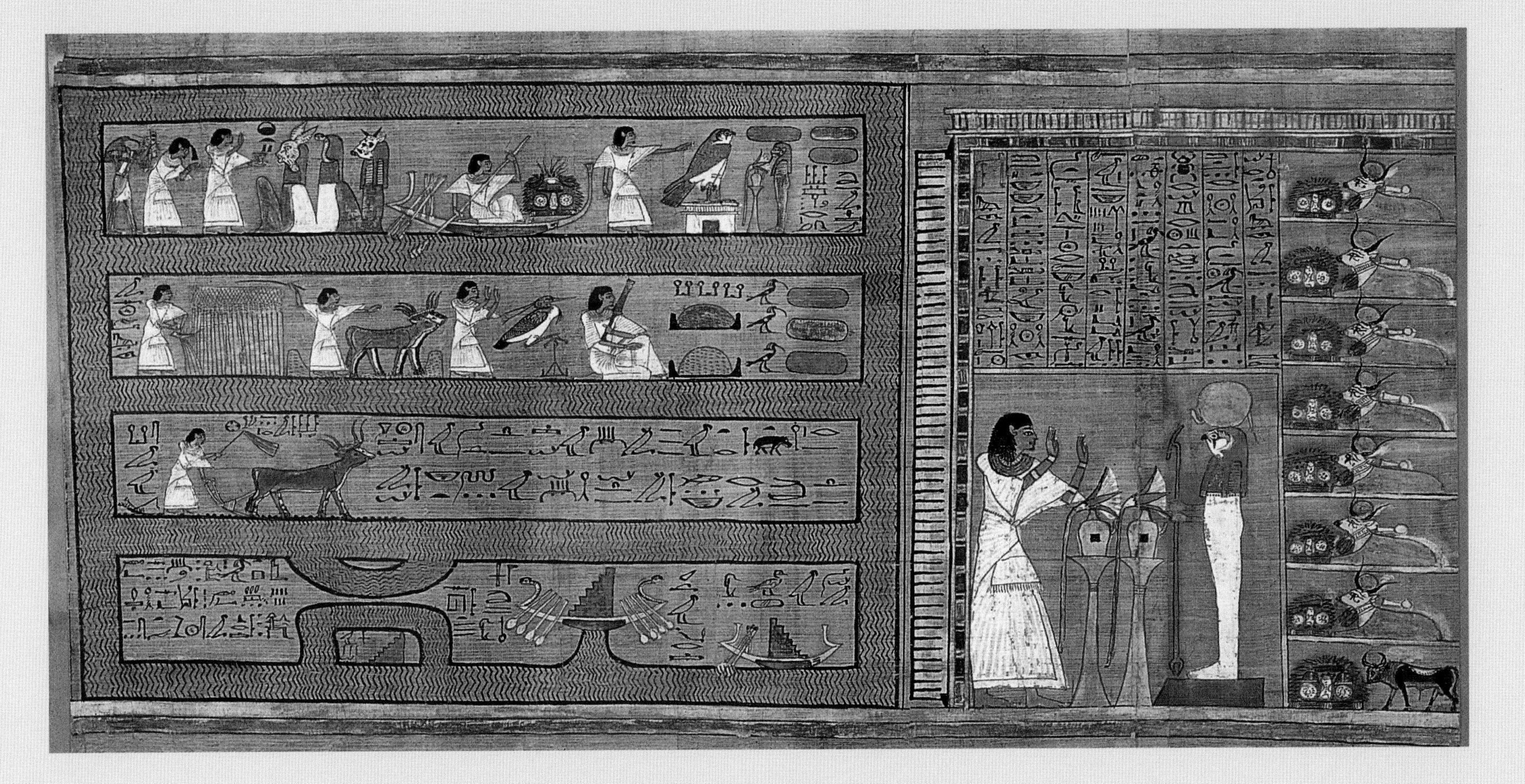

pure lotus flower that has ascended by the sunlight and is at the nose of the sun god, Re. I am the pure lotus that ascends upward." The lotus opening its petals at dawn symbolized the morning sun emerging from the darkness of night, and, similarly, life arising from the darkness of death.

Funerary texts present several conceptions of paradise. Thus the deceased may inhabit the underworld with Osiris; or rise up to the heavens to become one of the Imperishable Stars; or join the sun god, Re, in his "Barque of the Millions" in its journey across the sky. Later myths incorporate the Re and Osiris stories, as the two gods meet each night in the underworld on the sun's voyage through the darkness. As with the various creation myths (see pages 38–39), the acceptance of a range of ultimate destinations for the deceased is typical of the Egyptians' tolerant and multi-faceted belief system.

CREATURES OF THE UNDERWORLD

The Egyptian underworld, or Duat, was home to many strange and marvelous beings. Some were benign, such as the blessed spirits of the dead (*akh*s, above, right) and the *shabti*s, mummy-like figurines that came to life in the tomb to act as servants in the afterlife (above, center). Aided by funerary texts and amulets, the recently dead fluttered through Duat as winged *ba* spirits (above, left) to the Hall of Osiris. Among the dangers en route were soul-hunting demons and a giant serpent, Apep, which nightly tried to devour the sun as it passed through Duat. Every night, the god Seth fended off the serpent (opposite). Other monsters included Ammut—a hybrid of crocodile, hippopotamus, and feline—that ate the hearts of the sinful (opposite).

THE VALLEY OF THE KINGS

As the sun sank into the Theban Hills on the western horizon, dead souls sank down into the eternal embrace of Hathor, goddess of the West, who was regularly shown emerging from the hillside at her sacred site of Deir el-Bahari. Here, the 11th-dynasty king Nebhepetre Mentuhotep II (ca. 2008–1957 BCE) was laid to rest in his tomb below his funerary temple, surrounded by six priestesses of the goddess, who would protect his spirit.

The later New Kingdom pharaohs, from Amenhotep I to Ramesses XI, also associated Deir el-Bahari with Hathor, but amended the earlier arrangement by constructing a separate temple and tomb; their funerary temples, which face the river, remain highly visible, whereas their hidden tombs were constructed in the valleys on the other side of the hills. The main valley—named after the kings who lie buried within its silent depths—is marked by the natural pyramid shape of the Theban Peak (right), a rock known to the Egyptians by the apt name of Meretseger, or "She who Loves Silence." The superbly decorated rock-cut tombs include the huge funerary chambers of Thutmose III, Amenhotep II, Horemheb, Sety II, and the later Ramesside kings. Favorite courtiers, such as Yuya and Thuya, were also occasionally buried here as a mark of honor.

GLOSSARY

akh A dead person's blessed, transfigured spirit, resulting from the successful merging of the *ka* (soul) and the *ba* (the winged spirit of the deceased).

ankh "Life," represented by the hieroglyph ☥, a sacred emblem also frequently employed as a decorative motif.

Book of the Dead, The Term used to describe a type of funerary text, usually written on papyrus, comprising more than two hundred spells for ensuring the deceased's proper burial and safe passage into the afterlife.

hieroglyph (Greek: "sacred carved letters") A picture or symbol representing an object, concept, or sound used for inscriptions in temples and tombs. A shorthand "hieratic" form was used for writing on papyrus.

Late Period The name given to the last period in which Egypt was ruled by native kings (664–332 BCE), with the exception of two periods of Persian rule (525–405 BCE and 343–332 BCE).

ma'at "Truth," or "order," a cosmic principle that, it was believed, should govern all human and divine actions; it was personified and revered in the form of the goddess Ma'at, guardian of truth, justice, and harmony.

***mastaba* (Arabic: "bench")** A type of rectangular tomb common for wealthy private burials from the Old Kingdom onward.

Middle Kingdom The name given to the second great flowering of Egyptian civilization, covering the 11th to 13th dynasties of pharaohs (ca. 2081–1630 BCE).

New Kingdom The name given to the third and greatest flowering of Egyptian civilization, covering the 18th to 20th dynasties of pharaohs (ca. 1539–1075 BCE).

Old Kingdom The name given to the first great flowering of Egyptian civilization, covering the 3rd to 6th dynasties of pharaohs (ca. 2625–2130 BCE).

Pharaoh The king of Egypt, a Greek term derived from the Egyptian *per-aa* ("Great House"), which originally referred to the royal palace but from the New Kingdom onward was also used to mean the ruler.

Ptolemaic Of or pertaining to the Greek dynasty founded by Ptolemy I in 310 BCE and ending in 30 BCE with the death of Cleopatra VII.

pylon The monumental entrance of an Egyptian temple.

Ramesside (Ramessid) **(1)** *adj.* Of or pertaining to the "Ramesside" Period, the 19th and 20th dynasties (ca. 1292–1075 bce), spanning the reigns of the pharaohs Ramesses I to Ramesses XI. **(2)** *n.* A pharaoh of the Ramesside Period.

uraeus The image of the sacred serpent, or cobra, which was set on the king's brow to spit in the eyes of his enemies.

wedjat A decorative motif in the form of the Eye of Horus, which was a symbol of the power of the falcon god. The *wedjat* was frequently worn as a protective amulet.

FOR MORE INFORMATION

The British Museum
Great Russell Street
London WC1B 3DG
+44 (0) 20 7323 8000/8299
Web site: http://www.britishmuseum.org
The British Museum houses the world's largest and most comprehensive collection of Egyptian antiquities outside the Egyptian Museum in Cairo.

Brooklyn Museum
Egyptian, Classical, and Ancient Middle Eastern Art
200 Eastern Parkway
Brooklyn, NY 11238-6052
(718) 638-5000
Web site: http://www.brooklynmuseum.org/collections/egyptian_classical_middle_eastern
The Brooklyn Museum's collection of ancient Egyptian art is one of the largest in the United States. The museum's Web site offers information about many artifacts and archaeological digs undertaken by the curatorial staff.

Carnegie Museum of Natural History
4400 Forbes Avenue
Pittsburgh, PA 15213
(412) 622-3131
Web site: http://www.carnegiemnh.org/exhibits/egypt
This museum's Walton Hall of Ancient Egypt includes rich examples of Egyptian culture and life.

Egyptian Museum
Midan El Tahrir
Cairo, Egypt 11557
(202) 578-2448; (202) 578-2452
Web site: http://www.egyptianmuseum.gov.eg
The Egyptian Museum in Cairo exhibits more than 120,000 objects from the prehistoric era to the Greco-Roman period.

EMuseum
Minnesota State University, Mankato
Web site: http://www.mnsu.edu/emuseum/prehistory/egypt
This Web site includes online information about ancient Egypt, including daily life, art, military, architecture, hieroglyphs, and government.

Freer Gallery of Art and Arthur M. Sackler Gallery
Smithsonian Institution
P.O. Box 37012, MRC 707
Washington, DC 20013-7012
(202) 633-1000
Web site: http://www.asia.si.edu
One of the Smithsonian Institution's museums located on the National Mall, the Freer includes Egyptian art in its collections.

Institute of Egyptian Art and Archaeology
University of Memphis
Jones Hall, Room 201
Memphis, TN 38152-3380
(901) 678-2555
Web site: http://www.memphis.edu/egypt/main.html
Established in 1984, this institute is devoted to the study of art and culture of ancient Egypt through research, exhibition, teaching, and community programs.

Royal Ontario Museum
100 Queen's Park
Toronto, ON M5S 2C6
Canada
Web site: http://www.rom.on.ca/schools/egypt/learn
The Web site of this Canadian museum offers information about mummification, hierglyphics, geography, religion, life , and culture in ancient Egypt.

Web Sites

Due to the changing nature of Internet links, Rosen Publishing has developed an online list of Web sites related to the subject of this book. This site is updated regularly. Please use this link to access this list:

http://www.rosenlinks.com/civ/egyp

FOR FURTHER READING

Aldred, C. *Egyptian Art*. London, England: Thames and Hudson, 1985.

Assmann, J. *Death and Salvation in Ancient Egypt*. Ithaca, NY: Cornell University Press, 2006.

Baines, J., and J. Malék. *Atlas of Ancient Egypt*. Oxford, England: Equinox, 1990.

Bard, K. *Introduction to the Archaeology of Ancient Egypt*. Malden, MA: Blackwell, 2007.

Brewer, D., and E. Teeter. *Egypt and the Egyptians*. Cambridge, England: Cambridge University Press, 2007.

Dunand, F., and C. Zivie-Coche. *Gods and Men in Egypt: 3000 BCE to 395 CE*. Ithaca, NY: Cornell University Press, 2004.

Fletcher, J. *The Egyptian Book of Living and Dying*. London, England: Duncan Baird Publishers, 2009.

Forman, W., and S. Quirke. *Hieroglyphs and the Afterlife in Ancient Egypt*. Norman, OK: University of Oklahoma Press, 1996.

Grajetzki, W. *The Middle Kingdom of Ancient Egypt: History, Archaeology and Society*. London, England: Duckworth, 2006.

Hart, G. *Egyptian Myths*. Austin, TX: University of Texas Press, 1997.

Hart, G. *The Routledge Dictionary of Egyptian Gods and Goddesses*. London, England: Routledge, 2005.

Hill, M., ed. *Gifts for the Gods: Images from Egyptian Temples*. New Haven, CT: Yale University Press, 2007.

Kemp, B. *Ancient Egypt: Anatomy of a Civilization*. London, England: Routledge, 2005.

Kemp, B. *100 Hieroglyphs: Think Like an Egyptian*. London, England: Granta, 2005.

Lehner, M. *The Complete Pyramids*. London, England: Thames and Hudson, 2008.

Lichteim, M. *Ancient Egyptian Literature*. 3 Vols. Berkeley, CA: University of California Press, 1980.

Nicholson, P., and I. Shaw. *Ancient Egyptian Materials and Technology*. Cambridge, England: Cambridge University Press, 1999.

Pemberton, D. *Treasures of the Pharaohs*. London, England: Duncan Baird Publishers, 2003.

Pinch, G. *Magic in Ancient Egypt*. Austin, TX: University of Texas Press, 1994.

Quirke, S. *Ancient Egyptian Religion*. London, England: British Museum Press, 1992.

Ray, J. D. *The Rosetta Stone and the Rebirth of Ancient Egypt*. Cambridge, MA: Harvard University Press, 2007.

Reeves, N., and R. Wilkinson. *The Complete Valley of the Kings: Tombs and Treasures of Egypt's Greatest Pharaohs*. London, England: Thames and Hudson, 2008.

Robins, G. *The Art of Ancient Egypt*. Cambridge, MA: Harvard University Press, 2000.

Romer, J. *Ancient Lives: the Story of the Pharaoh's Tombmakers*. London, England: Weidenfeld & Nicolson, 1984.

Romer, J. *The Great Pyramid: Ancient Egypt Revisited*. Cambridge, England: Cambridge University Press, 2007.

Russmann, E. R., N. Strudwick, and T. G. H. James. *Temples and Tombs: Treasures of Egyptian Art from the British Museum*. Seattle, WA: Washington University Press, 2005.

Shaw, I., ed. *The Oxford History of Ancient Egypt*. Oxford, England: Oxford University Press, 2004.

Shaw, I., and P. Nicholson. *The Princeton Dictionary of Ancient Egypt*. Princeton, NJ: Princeton University Press, 2008.

Silverman, David P., ed. *Ancient Egypt*. New York, NY: Oxford University Press, 1997.

Simpson, W. K., ed. *The Literature of Ancient Egypt: An Anthology of Stories, Instructions, and Poetry*. New Haven, CT: Yale University Press, 2003.

Smith, W. Stevenson. *The Art and Architecture of Ancient Egypt*. New Haven, CT: Yale University Press, 1999.

Strouhal, E. *Life in Ancient Egypt*. Cambridge, England, and Norman, OK: Cambridge University Press and University of Oklahoma Press, 1992.

Taylor, J. H. *Death and the Afterlife in Ancient Egypt*. Chicago, IL: University of Chicago Press, 2001.

Wilkinson, R. H. *The Complete Gods and Goddesses of Ancient Egypt*. London, England: Thames and Hudson, 2003.

Wilkinson, R. H. *The Complete Temples of Ancient Egypt*. London, England: Thames and Hudson, 2000.

Wilkinson, R. H. *Reading Egyptian Art: A Hieroglyphic Guide to Ancient Egyptian Painting and Sculpture*. London, England: Thames and Hudson, 1999.

Wilkinson, T., ed. *The Egyptian World*. London, England: Routledge, 2007.

Wilkinson, T. *Lives of the Ancient Egyptians*. London, England: Thames and Hudson, 2007.

INDEX

E

F

G

H

ABOUT THE AUTHOR

Dr. Joann Fletcher teaches Egyptian archaeology at the University of York and as part of the university's Mummy Research Group has examined human remains around the world. She is also Egyptologist for Harrogate Museums and Arts, and as a consultant to the media makes regular television appearances, most recently as lead investigator in the History Channel series *Mummy Forensics*. Her publications include *The Egyptian Book of Living and Dying*; *Cleopatra the Great*; *The Search for Nefertiti*; *Alexander the Great: Son of the Gods*; *Egypt's Sun King: Amenhotep III*; and *Oils and Perfumes of Ancient Egypt*, along with contributions to several guide books and the BBC's History Web site.

PICTURE CREDITS

PICTURE CREDITS

The publisher would like to thank the following people, museums, and photographic libraries for permission to reproduce their material. Every care has been taken to trace copyright holders. However, if we have omitted anyone, we apologize and will, if informed, make corrections in any future editions.

Abbreviations

t top; **c** center; **b** bottom; **l** left; **r** right

AKG: AKG London
AR: Art Resource, New York
BAL: Bridgeman Art Library, London/New York
BM: British Museum, London (Egyptian Antiquities)
CM: The Egyptian Museum, Cairo
ET: ET Archive, London
JL: Jürgen Liepe, Berlin
RHPL: Robert Harding Picture Library, London
WFA: Werner Forman Archive, London

Cover Tony Stone Images/John Lawrence; **3** AKG; **4** Tony Stone/Jeremy Horner; **5** Axiom/James Morris; **6** Erich Lessing/AR; **7** WFA; **8** JL/CM (JE10062); **10** JL/CM (JE 95254); **11** JL/CM (JE14276+89661); **12–13** Graham Harrison; **14–15b** JL/CM (JE 34571); **15l** JL/CM (JE 46694); **15r** AKG/Erich Lessing; **16** Bildarchiv Preussischer Kulturbesitz/AR; **18** WFA/Schultz Collection, New York; **19** BM (EA10470); **20** BM (EA24); **21** Michael Holford/BM; **22** JL/CM (JE 64735); **24–25** Martyn Rose; **26** BAL; **27** BAL/BM; **28** AKG/Louvre, Paris; **29** AKG/Erich Lessing; **30** WFA; **32** Scala/AR; **33** AKG/Erich Lessing; **34** Axiom/James Morris; **36** BAL/Giraudon/Louvre, Paris; **38** Michael Holford; **39** AKG/Erich Lessing/Kunsthistorisches Museum, Vienna; **40** Tony Stone/Stuart Westmorland; **41** BAL/Giraudon/Louvre, Paris; **42** BAL/Giraudon/CM; **44–45** Chris Caldicott; **46–47** Axiom/James Morris; **46t** JL/CM (JE 36143); **47t** Tony Stone Images/Jessica Johnson; **50** Joann Fletcher; **51** AKG/Erich Lessing/CM; **52** JL/CM (JE 43566); **53** Ancient Art & Architecture Collection; **54–55** RHPL; **56** Tony Stone Images/Ary Diesendruck; **57** Tony Stone Images/Tom Till; **58** JL/CM (JE 32018); **59** BAL/ Giraudon/CM; **60** Chris Caldicott; **61** Scala/AR; **62–63** Chris Caldicott; **64** Werner Forman/AR; **65** WFA/E Strouhal; **66** Images Colour Library; **67** ET/CM; **68** Erich Lessing/AR; **69** RHPL/Ellen Rooney; **71** Henri Stierlin; **72** AKG; **73** Tony Stone Images/David Higgs; **74** JL/CM (JE 44951); **75** Powerstock Zefa; **77** BAL/Giraudon; **78** JL/CM (JE 40679); **79** WFA; **80–81** Tony Stone Images/John Lawrence; **82** Michael Holford/BM; **83** JL/CM (JE 30875); **84** Graham Harrison/BM; **85** JL/CM (JE 61467); **86–87** Chris Caldicott; **90** JL/CM (JE 6259a); **91** BAL/Giraudon; **93l** BM (EA 7876); **93r** WFA/ Staatliche Museum zu Berlin Agyptisches Museum; **94–95** Powerstock Zefa ; **96** Tony Stone Images/Purdy Matthews; **97** Staatliche Museum zu Berlin Agyptisches Museum (INV 9583 10176); **98** JL/CM (JE 44861); **99** BAL/Giraudon; **100** Joann Fletcher; **101** Joann Fletcher; **102** WFA/Louvre, Paris; **103** Scala, Florence; **104–105** Tony Stone Images/Richard Passmore; **106** RHPL/Julia Bayne; **107** Joann Fletcher; **108** ET/Louvre, Paris; **109** Axiom/James Morris; **110–111** ©The Trustees of the British Museum/AR; **112** ET/BM; **113** BM (11836, 64592, 22992, 57733, 64593, 65515); **114** ET; **116** Graham Harrison; **117** AKG; **118** Michael Holford; **119** Werner Forman/AR; **122** NILE; **123** ET/CM; **124** Ancient Art and Architecture Collection; **125** BAL/Giraudon/CM; **126–27** BM (EA 9901/3); **128** JL/CM (JE 46724); **129** AKG/BM; **131c** JL/CM (CG 48406); **132–33** RHPL/ John Ross.